THE *flip·flop* CEO®

6th Printing

ISBN: 978-0-9864259-0-5

Cover designed by: SeaSaw Marketing
Interior designed by: Claire Fontana

Visit us on the web:
TheFlipFlopCEO.com

What Readers Are Saying

BOB PROCTOR
Public Speaker, Author
Featured in *The Secret*

Probably the only thing stopping you from living the life you love is your paradigm. Your paradigm is your current way of thinking—your habitual way of acting, which is creating the life that you are presently experiencing. When you change your paradigm, you change your results. The Flip-Flop CEO will help you make one of the biggest paradigm shifts of your life, by walking you through all of the reasons why network marketing is such a brilliant business model to live your dream.

Here are points to look at closely before you begin network marketing:

1. Make sure you are joining a good company with strong leadership.
2. Make certain the company has a good product, a product you are proud to represent.
3. Make certain the person signing you up has the talent, experience, and desire to properly train you. And if they don't, ask to speak to their upline and ask them if they will properly launch you in the business.

Network marketing is a tremendous way to get into business for yourself and it is the most moral form of compensation in business today. There is no nepotism, games, or favorites, you earn exactly what you are worth to your organization.

"I love this sassy informative new book about the business of network marketing. It's the best book I have read so far which authentically explains how regular people can live a life of freedom and choices, happy healthy lives, while building a business which can produce CEO income—all while wearing your flip-flops! I have been sharing with everyone in my life that there is a way out of the rat race. Lory and Janine devour a subject which so many out there do not fully understand."

— **Danielle D.**

"This is the best book I have ever read that is for everyone to understand this amazing profession!"

— **Diane P.**

"This book took all my thoughts about network marketing, put them on paper, and then set me straight. Reading the truth and facts as well as the success stories was so helpful, enlightening,

What Readers Are Saying

and inspiring. I would recommend this book to anyone thinking about jumping into this profession or give it to those who think your decision is a bad idea. They don't know what they are talking about."

— **Heather S.**

"Amazing! A must-read for anyone in network marketing, skeptics included!"

— **Lisa Vetter**

"Great read for the beginner network marketer!"

— **Carrie Kirby**

"If you ever wondered or are slightly skeptical—this is a smart read. There is a better way to live... in flip-flops!"

— **Janel French**

"Very informative! Loved this book and its perspective."

— **C.K.**

"Loved it. Great book that explains why we all need network marketing as a Plan B. No matter if we have a full-time job that we work five days a week, we all have time seven days a week to put a little time into a network marketing gig and have something to fall back on, or just to build something for the future. Easy to read. Really loved this book. Thanks."

— **Amazon Customer**

"Two thoughts occurred to me as I read this book. First, I have stepped one toe into network marketing with a company that is a perfect fit for my existing business. I wonder what would happen if I actually dedicated some time to it? Second, this business is perfect for my niece! I got her a copy of this book as soon as I finished reading it."

— **Laura Orsini**

Acknowledgements

From Lory and Janine:

Since embracing this business, our lives have been filled with so many inspirational, powerful, and compassionate friends. Because of all of you, we've gotten a glimpse of what is possible in this world. We're forever grateful to be a part of such a life-changing community. We are truly better together.

Whitney, you are exactly what we were searching for! You immediately caught the vision, immersed yourself in the experience, and became a passionate advocate of this profession. Thank you for putting your whole self into this project to authentically communicate our voice. We admire your sass, wisdom, and dedication. Thank you for making our dream a reality.

Dane, you are a part of who we are and everything we do. We adore you. Without you, Melissa Linden, and Debbie Onsager, this book might not have been written. Each of you have been our angels along the way. Thank you for being our sounding board, with your unwavering commitment to support us in speaking our truth. Words cannot adequately convey our appreciation for your unconditional love, guidance, and honesty. We cherish your friendship.

To our Shower Curtain Girls—Dana Eriksson, Jen Furrier, Andrea Scholer, Debi Tombazian, and Kerri Laryea—thank you for insisting that there was a book within us and a story that had to be told.

To Bevla, thank you for knowing that Whitney was the one.

To Jodi Low and Renee Dee for inspiring our dream. Thank you, girlfriends!!

For sharing your incredible love and light, thank you, Dr. Tanda Cook, Dr. Sarah Marshall, Jesse Neidt, Roxanne Melker, Melissa Haupt, and Chrissa Michelle.

We are also so grateful to all of our friends, including everyone mentioned above, who took the time to read our book and provide invaluable feedback ... Hope Baker, Stasia Trivison, Valerie Edwards, Iain Pritchard, Jill Ellis, Audra Berger, Diane Ryan, Jill Lohmiller, Tom and Lorraine Callaghan, Catherine Swinscoe, Doreen Bishop, Billie Young, Melissa Krieger, Kendra Katter, Crystal Barcello, Donna Price, Ericka Hirons, Jessica Emes, Chantelle Braham, Jamie Wieferich, Cathy Swann, Carrie Severson, Bobcat Brown, Melinda Adams-Johnson, Shari Weller, Kim Mylls, Jodi Towns, Geri Amster, Barbeth Pinkney, Meg McPhinney, Todd Hill, Rosemary Price, and Gayle Kelly. We appreciate you more than our words could possibly express!

We also want to thank each one of you who shared your story

with us for our book. What an inspiring group of leaders you are. Thank you all for exemplifying what is possible when belief and commitment collide!

Doug and Marcus, you are the wind beneath our wings. Marcus, you are the best dad in the whole world. Thank you for every second that you spent taking such good care of Parker and Hudson when Mommy and TaTa couldn't be there. Doug, thank you for your wisdom and tireless support. We appreciate all of the sacrifices you've made so that our book could be written. We love the "big" and "little" men in our lives with all of our hearts!

From Whitney:

Lory and Janine, thank you for sharing your vision, your hearts, and your lives with me. It is such an honor to be a part of this project. Lory, you blazed a trail that a lot of us walk on today. Thanks for having the courage to stick with it.

To Laura Russell, Jamie Rubin, Anjuli Fiedler, and Pamela Spycher, thank you for being such great friends, and for taking the time to review the book. Your feedback was priceless.

Bevla, thank you for being the bright, beautiful magnet that brought us all together. You are one of a kind.

I am very blessed to have a group of comrades and loved ones who not only support me in my zany endeavors, they join me in them. They are my mastermind group, book editors, vacation buddies, business partners, and best friends. To Ramona, Samara, Kate, Christina, Blythe, and Rob, thank you for sharing this journey with me. I freakin' love you guys.

The trajectory of my life changed for the better when I stumbled upon this project, and the business model of network marketing. I have the heavens to thank for that.

To all of our book readers, thank you for putting up with this little yearbook signing. If you're shocked or offended by anything in the book, I take full responsibility for it.

Foreword

Each of us is the CEO of our own life (not just our profession). We have the choice of how we spend our money as well as how we spend our time. We can fill our schedules with activities that are fun, fulfilling, and financially rewarding, or with activities that hold us back. Are your choices of your current career or how you are spending your time getting in the way of achieving both the success and significance you deserve?

The Flip Flop CEO brings clarity to the often misunderstood field of network marketing, explaining its opportunity for prosperity while addressing and debunking the negative thoughts that surround it.

No matter how much you earn at your job, whether it be as a physician, an attorney, a hair stylist, or a receptionist, you are most likely trading time for money. Ask yourself, if you stop working, will you stop earning? This book shares a time-tested and realistic way for anyone who has the desire and motivation to seize the opportunity to begin earning residual income without the risk or capital required by most other options.

If you are looking for a lifestyle that allows you the freedom and flexibility to work around your life—rather than planning your life around your work—this book reveals it.

If you feel that you have to sacrifice a life of significance in order to have success, you might be surprised by what you'll learn from this little book.

Whether you are hoping to earn a little extra income, replace your six-figure salary, or create a plan B to help take you into retirement, be open to the possibility that the solution you're looking for may "look" very different than you thought! This book will explain how personal freedom and financial success are possible for you!

To your success!

Sharon Lechter, CPA CGMA

Founder & CEO, **Pay Your Family First**

Co-Author of the international bestseller, *Rich Dad Poor Dad*, and 14 other books in the Rich Dad series.

Co-Author of *Think and Grow Rich: Three Feet from Gold* and *Outwitting the Devil*

Author of *Save Wisely, Spend Happily*

When you change the way you look at things,
the things you look at change.

Wayne Dyer

A Flip-Flop CEO:

Doesn't do alarm clocks, bosses, or cubicles.
Makes up her own mind.
Thinks in terms of possibilities, not probabilities.
Lives her life by design.
Doesn't do hourly or salary.
Makes money and a difference... in her flip-flops.
She plans her work around her life...
rather than her life around her work!

Table of Contents

Introduction

We are mother and daughter. So naturally, we don't always agree.

In fact, the biggest bone of contention in our relationship to date is what inspired this book—the subject of network marketing. It came into our lives over ten years ago, when one of us decided to pursue it with gusto and the other resisted it with all her might. We battled for over a year.

Eventually, after lots of arguments, tears, and silence, we landed in a place where we finally saw eye to eye. Today, we've both built thriving network marketing businesses and have fulfilled many of our lifelong dreams, the biggest of which is working together.

We wrote this book because, while the divide in our perspectives of this profession is now bridged, it still exists in other families, friendships, and society at large. On one side are the insiders—people who believe in the business model, hopeful of the possibilities it presents, frustrated that others don't see it. On the other are the outsiders—skeptical of all the promises, annoyed and offended that it keeps showing up. In the middle are the people who have *absolutely no idea what it is*.

Wherever you stand, this book is for you. And there are a couple of things we hope you get out of reading it. The first is a brand new outlook on the network marketing profession. The second, and most important, is a heartfelt realization that you can have more, and *deserve more*, in your life than others claim is possible.

Our message may seem tough in parts, but we promise it truly comes from a place of love. So if we sound a little feisty, it's because we're fired up about this topic. We know that when most people hear the words "network marketing," they instantly plug their ears, and we didn't want to get tuned out.

When we decided that this book needed to be written, we went in search of someone who could help communicate our voice. We found the perfect fit in the form of an entrepreneur, writer, and recovering attorney, who ironically despised network marketing. But there are no accidents. She became not only a believer, but an advocate for network marketing, as well.

We don't claim to be experts on the subject of network marketing. We're just living proof that it *does* work, and you *can* have it all: a career and a life on your own terms. This profession has given us the gift of a lifetime—the ability to plan our work around our lives rather than our lives around our work. And now we want to share that gift, in the form of this book, with you.

Our complete stories can be found in the Afterword. Inspirational stories from other Flip-Flop CEOs can be found at the end of the book.

CHAPTER ONE

Get a Life

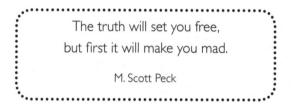

> The truth will set you free,
> but first it will make you mad.
>
> M. Scott Peck

We don't mean to be rude, but don't you think your life could use a facelift?

We're guessing you'd rather get a colonoscopy than go to work tomorrow. The last time you felt well-rested was in high school. Your salary doesn't budge. Your bonuses are abysmal—or nonexistent. Your retirement fund has gone from being a nest egg to a goose egg, and your couch has more money than your savings account.

Sound familiar?

Day in and day out, you fume in rush hour traffic while you cuddle your espresso instead of your kids. You drag your laptop on vacation and your phone to the gym. You're a prisoner to your list of things to do. You have money, but no time. Or time, but no money. And you are tragically un-fun.

But that's not the worst part.

The worst part is that unless you make a move, nothing will change. Tomorrow will be the same as today. Next week will be the same as tomorrow. Unless, of course, there's a massive recession looming—then it could get even worse.

Don't shoot the messengers! We just want to help. We want you to know that you have options.

We're not talking about a second job. We're not talking about winning the lottery. We're not talking about "doing what you love and expecting the money to follow." (That only worked for Oprah.)

We're talking about something you've probably heard of before, something you might have dismissed until now, something lurking right under your nose. We're talking about network marketing.

Yes, we said it—network marketing.

Now, we're not stupid. We know that network marketing still gets a bad rap, and that you'd rather take on a paper route than be caught doing it. We see from your license plate that you've earned a degree. We know you have a fancy title and an image to uphold and that your job—even though you don't love it—makes you feel like you have at least a *little* stability in your life. Not to mention that you finally have your own personal parking space, a spot in the fridge, and you've got your cubicle decorated just the way you like it.

Don't worry, we felt the same way not that long ago. In fact, prior to doing our research on network marketing, we were some of the biggest haters and skeptics around. Let's face it, the profession does have a checkered past, and some network marketers still make the whole place look like a carnival. But that's not a good enough reason to be deterred.

That's not a reason to dismiss what could be a viable and credible financial opportunity for *you*.

Trust us, we've done it all. We've been corporate rat-racers, passionate entrepreneurs, and loyal employees. We've had careers we loved with salaries we hated, and careers we hated with salaries we loved. So believe us when we say that network marketing is one of the greatest ways to earn a buck.

We wrote this book not to convince you, but to inform you— to flip your frame of reference about a profession that is gravely misunderstood. We wrote this book because we want you to get a life, and a *good* one at that.

CHAPTER TWO

Get a Clue

I'd rather have 1% of 100 people's efforts than 100% of my own.

John Paul Getty

Most people have some idea of what network marketing is. At least, they think they do. In reality their knowledge is about as up-to-date as a perm, but we'll get to that later.

Network marketing, also known as multi-level marketing, is a system for marketing and distributing products. It's essentially word-of-mouth advertising.

Companies that use network marketing systems are really no different from other companies, except for how they make their products known. Instead of investing in billboards, fancy magazine spreads, celebrity endorsements, and giant ad agencies, they spend most of their dollars on people. Yep, that's right—they pay *people* to spread the word. And rather than invest in pricey distributors, middlemen, and retail space to get the goods from A to B (say, a can of soda from plant to consumer), they again use people, or nowadays, allow purchases to be made online.

Before the Internet was invented, network marketing was a different animal altogether. Because there was no such thing as e-commerce, people in network marketing companies acted as virtual storefronts, either going from door to door or person to person to move a product. It was time consuming and often annoying. Network marketers also had to purchase the products ahead of time, which meant they were left with the burdens of inventory and delivery.

Today, consumers are cyber-savvy and enjoy buying things online. So with network marketing, they hear about a product from a person who actually uses it, maybe check out a sample, and a mouse-click later, they're done. The products go directly from company to doorstep. Services are the same as goods— someone learns about it, goes online, signs up for the service and *poof!*, it's delivered. All the network marketer does is make the recommendations and connections.

Many experts believe that network marketing is one of the fastest and most efficient ways for a company to move a product. If you think about it, that makes sense. How fast does your online social network grow? How soon after a rumor gets started does the entire office know the scoop?

Well, that's how fast a company can reach the masses with network marketing.

With that kind of market penetration, it's no wonder that the profession does $183.7 billion in global sales a year.

Even some of the world's most well-known corporations—including Jockey, Citigroup, Sprint, Verizon—and the most successful entrepreneurs—including Donald Trump and Warren Buffet—are venturing into the network marketing world.

Let's face it: newspapers are quickly becoming obsolete; commercials are getting lost in fast forward; pop-up ads are being ignored. What that means is that companies are desperate for innovative ways to reach their buyers. Turns out, the age-old practice of telling a friend still reigns supreme.

Businesses aren't the only ones that like network marketing.

Consumers like it, too. That's because, typically, the products are of higher quality than their retail counterparts.

Since the companies are redirecting their marketing and distribution budgets, they can afford to create better products while paying their network marketers impressive incomes. And who doesn't love better products?

How Network Marketers Get Paid

The only people who love network marketing more than the companies and customers are the network marketers themselves. Also known as independent distributors/business owners, consultants, or representatives, these are the people who get paid to spread the word. And *how* they get paid is pretty cool.

Although it varies among companies, in general, a network marketer—let's call her Lisa—gets paid a percentage of all the goods bought by people she referred to the company. That's the *first part*. These people aren't in the business of network marketing—they're just customers of the company who were referred by Lisa. And in some cases, Lisa wouldn't even complete the transaction herself. Instead, she would introduce her friends to the products and refer them to the website, where they can shop by themselves.

In that respect, it's a lot like direct selling (of encyclopedia and vacuum fame), but revolutionized by the World Wide Web.

So let's review. For now, Lisa gets paid to talk about products she loves. Nice.

But that's not the best part. The best part about network marketing is that Lisa also gets paid a commission on purchases made by people she hasn't personally talked to at all.

Let us explain.

Like we said, in network marketing, a consultant is compensated for the purchases made by their own referrals.

But they can also earn commissions on the purchases made by their *network's* referrals as well. That means if Lisa connects four people to the business, and they each do the same, Lisa will have twenty-one people in her network, including herself. And she will get paid on each and every referral those twenty-one people make in *addition* to her own. In most network marketing companies, she can even get paid on her network's personal purchases, too, as they become part of her group volume.

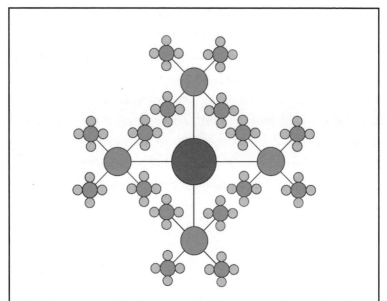

This is an example of a network of representatives. When Lisa joins the business, she will be at the center of her network. Anyone who later joins her team will be in her network, and at the center of their own network.

As you can see, this math can go on and on. Anyone can continue the referral process (three more, five more, ten more), and as a result, Lisa's network of independent reps and happy shoppers will expand. Over time, she can actually be compensated for the purchases of hundreds or even thousands of people.

And that's the power of a network. That, my friends, is *leverage*.

If real estate is about location, location, location, then network marketing is about *leverage, leverage, leverage*. Leverage is about investing in something once, and getting paid for it again and again. Investors have *leverage*—their money grows money on its own. The founder of a restaurant franchise has leverage—she built a template for one business, but gets paid on ten more. An entrepreneur who automates a system has leverage—an hour's worth of work saved him fifty. And network marketers have leverage—they can have five conversations about a product, and get paid for five thousand. They can train a tiny team of people, and end up with an army.

So if network marketing is so great, why in the world isn't everyone doing it? Oh boy, where do we start?

First off, we know what you're thinking: This sounds like a pyramid scheme. No, we're not psychic. We've just been around this block before.

So let's get to that right now.

> In the past I've written songs for artists including Tina Turner, Smokey Robinson, Meatloaf, Cher and Michael Jackson. After 17 years of being a stay-at-home mom, I was a dinosaur in the music business and was at an age where most people start to retire. Owning a network marketing business is like having an insurance policy that pays out while you and your loved ones are still alive to enjoy it. You're building an asset that grows over time-and can create wealth beyond your wildest dreams.
>
> Sue Cassidy, Network Marketer

Get the Facts

- The Direct Selling Association, which also represents network marketing companies, recently celebrated its 100th anniversary. [i]

- As of 2015, 20.2 million people are registered network marketers in the United States. [ii]

- As of 2015, 103 million people are registered network marketers worldwide. [iii]

- United States online retail sales will grow from $225.5 billion in 2012 to $434.2 billion in 2017. Online retail sales will grow at a compound annual rate of 10% from 2012-2017. [iv]

- In 2015, according to the Adobe's Digital Index, total online sales on Cyber Monday rose yet another 16 percent from the prior year to $3.07 billion. [v]

- Mobile sales also reached a sales volume record in 2015, with $799 million of online spending coming from a smartphone or tablet. [v]

- According to ChannelAdvisor, in 2015 Amazon's Cyber Monday revenues increased 21.1 percent from the prior year, outperforming overall online sales growth of 18 percent. [v]

CHAPTER THREE

Get With the Times

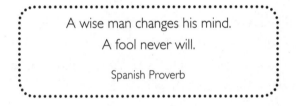

A wise man changes his mind.
A fool never will.

Spanish Proverb

Network marketing is probably about as controversial as politics, and people's opinions of it are just as fierce. The problem is, the majority of those opinions are based in *fiction*, not fact. And often in rumors that are decades old.

So let's cover the main objections about network marketing, and get to the root of this grapevine once and for all.

#1: It's a Pyramid Scheme

The instant people hear about network marketing, the first thing out of their mouths is, *"Isn't that one of those pyramid things?"*

For whatever reason, despite the fact that it's a Wonder of the World, when the majority of people think of a pyramid, they think scam. It's true. Never before—in the history of our society—have people been so afraid of a triangle.

So, why is the word "pyramid" so taboo? After all, most successful organizations are shaped like a pyramid. Our military, government, universities, corporations, hospitals, and school systems: all pyramids. And there's a reason for that. As an organizational structure of hierarchy, it's one of the strongest and most sustainable around. *Pyramids* are good.

Pyramid *schemes*, however, are not.

Most people think a pyramid scheme is an organization where one person (or a few) sits at the top making all the money, while the masses at the bottom do all the work, right? *Wrong.* That's not a pyramid scheme. *That's the company you work for.* And that's perfectly legal. Think about it: How many employees make more than their managers or CEO?

Legitimate network marketing companies don't look anything like that. In a network marketing company, all people start at the exact same place, but excel at different rates. *Anyone* can make it to the top. For some people, it takes months to get there, for others, it takes years. Some never do. Either way, it has nothing to do with *when* you signed up or *who* referred you. Many of the top earners of network marketing companies are people who got in decades after the company was established, and long after the first person to sign up. More importantly, many are earning far more than the person who referred them.

Say what?

That's right. The biggest misconception about network marketing is that the person who referred you (often called a "sponsor") is in a permanent position to ride your coattails all the way to the bank. But that is entirely false. In almost all network marketing companies, if your efforts outshine your sponsor's, you can pass or leapfrog right over him. That means *you can earn a better title, and a lot more dough.*

Just how is that possible? Well, the answer lies in the pie chart on page 58.

Network marketing companies make a set amount of money per product or service. That means there's only a certain amount of profit to go around. If they had to pay dozens of layers of network marketers, they'd go broke. So at some point, the commissions taper off.

The good news is that the resulting system is totally fair. Your sponsor cannot reach your *entire* network, or profit from *all* of your income. Of course, she will always get some form of compensation—after all, *she* made the referral. But the only person who can eat all of your pie is you.

Got that? Good.

Now, let's look at the difference between a legitimate network marketing company and a pyramid scheme.

Pyramid Scheme: Type One

The first type of pyramid scheme is actually called a Ponzi scheme (named for the criminal who made it famous). It doesn't involve a product, service, or even a business at all. It's just a scam described as an investment opportunity.

In a Ponzi scheme, the initial people who invest are paid from the subsequent investments of *other* people who later join the scheme. In other words, no genuine profit is made; the money is earned from brand new, unsuspecting members. Eventually, as the scheme becomes popular (remember, a few people *do* actually make money), the number of people entering at the *bottom* of the scheme exceeds the number of people sitting at the *top* of the scheme—hence the pyramid shape. The result is significant profit for the people who got in first, and anyone else who rises to the top before the scheme collapses.

With Ponzi schemes, since no business is involved, no real sale is made, and no security is traded, it's considered a scam.

If this is starting to sound familiar, it's because you've probably seen something similar before. Remember the chain letter you got as a kid—the one asking you to send a dollar (or in our case, ladies, a cute new pair of panties) to the person at the top of the list? Same deal. Illegal.

Eventually, Ponzi schemes are discovered and dismantled, which leaves the innocent people at the bottom in a monetary (or lingerie) deficit. The most tragic example of this was the Bernie Madoff scandal—yes, a Ponzi scheme—where thousands of people were defrauded to the tune of $50 billion.

Pyramid Scheme: Type Two

The second type of pyramid scheme is one in which a product or service exists, but is really just a cover for the scam itself. In reality, the products are never actually used. The company makes very little profit from the sale of these goods, but instead derives *almost all* of its revenue from the enrollment fees of new recruits. The representatives get paid for bringing new people into the scheme, as opposed to sales products that are consumed by individuals who are outside of the distribution network. In that sense, it's a lot like a Ponzi scheme, but with some meaningless (and often overpriced) products changing hands.

Legitimate Network Marketing Companies

Legitimate network marketing companies are completely different. They sell real products and services that are actually in demand. They do not compensate their network marketers for recruitment *alone*. There are no direct kickbacks from sign-up fees, and reps are only paid when a sale is made to an end user, or products are personally consumed (we're allowed to buy from ourselves).

So as you can see, at a distance, network marketing companies can look similar to pyramid schemes, but up close, they are dramatically different.

The confusion between pyramid schemes and network marketing companies is, in part, what created the stigma of the profession as a whole. That's because, when the network marketing profession was born, it was highly unregulated. Any old scammer could start a company, invent a product, funnel it through a "network marketing" channel, exaggerate product claims, and promise their recruits millions—with nothing to back it up. Unfortunately, that's exactly what many of them did. As a result, they opened and closed their doors in a matter of months, leaving a lot of casualties in their wake.

On top of that, con artists who didn't have the capital to

start their own businesses jumped into existing companies as independent representatives, and immediately began implementing fraudulent schemes of their own, many of which the companies themselves were not aware of. So in sum, there were *slimy* network marketing companies, and *legitimate* network marketing companies with slimy reps. It was the Wild West.

Around this time, our society wasn't sophisticated about these business models, so many otherwise intelligent people took the bait—hook, line, and sinker. To make matters worse, the buy-ins to join were generally larger than they are today. That's because, without the Internet, people had to acquire a significant amount of product at the outset in order to have inventory to sell. In other words, when people lost, they lost *big*. The result was that disgruntled reps were left with mountains of product they couldn't unload, debt they couldn't repay, and relationships they couldn't repair. So they did what any decent person would do in that situation—they warned all of their friends to stay away.

As a result of the mess, the Federal Trade Commission finally intervened and sued the bigger network marketing companies over a number of issues, including the legitimacy of the business model itself. At the end of the day, the courts declared that network marketing was a *completely legal way of distributing goods*, but the damage was done. A few bad apples had spoiled it for the bunch, and more than thirty years later, many people are still not up to date.

Today, the profession has far more regulation than it did thirty years ago. There are trade associations and watchdog groups galore. Problems still exist, but fortunately, most of them are practice specific and not industry-wide. But, as with anything—the stock market, a franchise, a marriage—you should do your due diligence before you get involved with a network marketing company. Trust us, no one wants more regulation in the network marketing profession than network marketers themselves. When the frauds and shady tactics are eliminated, we'll all have an easier time doing business.

If you're still skeptical, do your research. The Direct Selling Association (www.dsa.org) is a great place to start. The only thing we ask is that you don't throw the baby out with the bath water. The Bernie Madoff scandal hasn't deterred people from investing in legitimate companies, right? Of course not. They're just digging deeper now before they do it. The same can be said for network marketing—don't let its controversial past cause you to overlook its future potential.

Pyramid Schemes vs. Legitimate NM Companies

A pyramid scheme relies on sham products that don't work, are of little value to the consumer, and are often overpriced.

A legitimate NM company offers products with legitimate societal demand which are valuable and competitively priced.

In a pyramid scheme, consultant commissions are paid purely for recruiting or there are direct kickbacks from enrollment fees.

In a legitimate NM company, consultant compensation is tied to product/service distribution and sales.

Pyramid schemes frequently require large enrollment fees and require big product buy-ins. The company and distributors profit from training resources.

Legitimate NM companies have low start-up costs. Companies and distributors do not derive profit from training resources.

So, let's review:

Pyramid = shape.

Pyramid scheme = scam.

Network marketing = legitimate.

Are we clear?

Do your homework and know the difference.

#2: You Have to Get in Early to be Successful

We have to admit, it's hard to respond to an objection about network marketing that we don't even understand. But we'll give it a try.

We often hear people say that they are resistant to network marketing, or a particular company, because it's just too late to get in—like they missed a boat that just set sail.

The biggest problem with this myth is that no one is able to define it. For example, how early is early? Three months? Three years? Three decades? In the grand scheme of things, if a company is first to adopt a trend that takes time to catch on in mainstream society, is it possible to ever be too late? What if a company is fifty years old with a product line that's brand new? Aren't you now *ahead* of the curve?

You see the dilemma.

Remember, network marketing is slow-growing compared to a Super Bowl commercial; it takes longer than thirty seconds for millions to receive the word. And even if a large percentage of the people have heard of a product, that doesn't mean they have heard about how great it is.

People watch trailers for movies all the time, but often only see the one a friend recommends. The entire world can be aware of a brand, but still not use it.

What we're saying is, early is relative. So unless everyone you've ever met is buying from, or involved with, the *exact same network marketing company*, and you have no plans to ever *meet new people or make new friends*, congratulations—you're right on time.

By the way, a few words of caution for those of you looking just to get in early. Network marketing companies suffer from the same growing pains as any other start-up or new business; a high percentage of them fold within the first few years. So look out, because when it comes to being an early bird, not everyone gets a worm.

> There's almost no difference in income potential between those who get in early and those who don't. And our society is so diverse that it doesn't really matter. There will always be people who want to take the risk with an unknown brand, hoping for the big reward, and people who want to wait until a company has established its credibility and financial security.
>
> Doris Wood, Founder, MLMIA
> (Multi-Level Marketing International Association)

#3: Saturation

This conspiracy theory is sort of a hybrid of the "getting in early" and "pyramid scheme" myths. The assumption behind it is that when the market becomes saturated with a particular product, the demand will run out. Or when the market gets saturated with salespeople, there will be a shortage of customers to go around.

Neither of these arguments has any merit. Sure, technically everyone could have a certain type of product, like a mattress, refrigerator, or computer. But that never eliminates the demand. Products get old; they need to be renewed, revised, and replaced. You don't see Apple discontinuing iPads just because everyone seems to have one. On the contrary, the company just becomes more innovative, inventing newer, better, and cooler models of the versions already released.

Network marketing companies are no different. In fact, few of them encounter this issue in the first place, because they *intentionally* get into industries where products need to be reordered. From vitamins to face creams to telephone service—the whole business is designed to bring the user back for more. They're no stranger to innovation either. You can bet that before a product gets tired, there's a newer, shinier one waiting in the wings.

And we suppose it's *hypothetically* possible for millions and millions of people to join the same network marketing company, but that also never happens. There are hundreds of network marketing companies to choose from; the idea that everyone will join the same one is sort of ludicrous. Besides, the population changes over time. Every day, a whole new crop of people turn eighteen and form a brand new consumer base. At the same time, a population of independent distributors and customers dies off. To suggest that in a short span of time, millions upon millions of people will all choose the same career is just crazy. Not only has that never happened in network marketing, it's never happened *at all*.

Saturation case = closed.

#4: I'm Not Like Those People

The good news is that network marketing is an equal opportunity business. The bad news is that network marketing is an equal opportunity business—*anyone* can get in. That's right—no education, degree, diploma, certificate, license, experience, resume, interview, references, IQ, or *ounce of class* required. All you need is a pulse and a social security number.

So, given this gigantic welcome mat, it's no surprise that network marketing can be a magnet for misfits, flunkies, sleazeballs, and buffoons. And it's also not shocking that these fools tarnish the profession with their obnoxious (and completely ineffec-tive) tactics once they get in. You know the ones—the innocent happy hour that turns into a sneak-attack business presentation, the person who saturates her Facebook page every hour with product claims and promotions, the cousin who harasses you with samples and turns your family reunion into an infomercial. You're not the only ones who've been victimized by this garbage before. We have, too.

> When network marketing is done the right way, it's not the same industry as the one most people are criticizing.
>
> Tim Sales, Network Marketing Expert, Author, and Trainer

But *wake up*—the fact that network marketing attracts a few weirdos has nothing to do with the legitimacy of the business model itself. More importantly, this fact has nothing to do with you.

Thomas Edison once said, "Who you are will show up in what you do." And network marketing is certainly no exception. If you're professional now, you'll be professional in network marketing. If you're cheesy now, you'll be cheesy in network marketing. If you are *completely ineffective* at life, you will be completely ineffective at network marketing. It's not rocket science, people. It's common sense.

Besides, these folks are not just in network marketing, they're in every business. They're just more noticeable in network marketing because it's a business that involves connecting with people. And we hate to break it to you, but if your cousin is acting like a stalker now that he's doing network marketing, that's not a network marketing problem. It's a *family* problem.

> Network marketing leaders are like athletic coaches. They are looking for people with talent, teach-ability, and great hearts.
>
> Dr. Tom Barrett, Author and Network Marketing Expert

Don't let a few fruit loops discourage you from considering a business model that is legitimate and fair. Trust us; you'll find lots of people in this business who are ethical, smart, and fun. Luckily the more you look, the more you'll find.

#5: It's Insincere

Ahhh…the dreaded kickback. How can we ever be sure that a referral is sincere when money is involved?

The answer is: we can't. It's just a fact of life—some people are genuine, others are not.

It's not like this is breaking news. You didn't really think that movie-star spokeswoman was actually using drugstore makeup, did you? Or that four out of five dentists *really* recommended that gum?

The point is, you're being marketed to every day—every time you log on to the Internet, click an affiliate link, watch a commercial, or join a referral-based network. Sure, it hurts more when a friend is insincere, but that doesn't mean network marketing is to blame. It means your friend picked the wrong products to represent, and you need to take that up with your friend.

Look, most people involved in network marketing are *sincerely* enthusiastic about the products they represent. In fact, a lot of them *became* reps for a company specifically to get a discount on their favorite products. With hundreds of network marketing companies to choose from, why on Earth would they choose one they didn't like?

Not only do most of them love the products, we can guarantee you they're fired up about the compensation plan as well. With everything we've told you about it so far, can you blame them? If you really loved what a product can do for your life, and you'd made a decent income just telling other people about it, wouldn't you be drinking the Kool-Aid, too?

Besides, we've pointed out that most of you already do network marketing anyway; you just didn't know it. The restaurant, boutique, or spa recommendation—that's network marketing. The dentist referral—network marketing. The movie your friends should watch, book they should read, song they should download—network marketing. Every day you spread the word for brands you love. *That's network marketing.*

So listen: if you're going to walk like a duck, act like a duck, and quack like a duck, shouldn't you get paid to *be* a duck?

You get the point.

#6: I Don't Have Time

This is by far the most underwhelming argument against network marketing we've ever heard.

There's no such thing as not having enough time for network

marketing. If you have time to read this book, you have time for network marketing. If you have time to tell your friends about a restaurant you love, you have time for network marketing. If you have time to complain about your job, you have time for network marketing. If you have time to surf the Internet, watch TV, or read the tabloids, you have time for network marketing. If you are so pressed for time that you can't do network marketing, you need a solution that will give you more time. *That* is network marketing.

#7: I Don't Want to Make Money off My Friends

A lot of people are resistant to network marketing because they don't want to "use their friends." But the stigma of network marketing doesn't come from people *using* their networks. It comes from people abusing their networks.

Network marketing isn't about asking your friends to buy products they don't need or spend money they don't have. It isn't about turning every happy hour or dinner party into a business meeting or pitch. It isn't about hounding or harassing time and time again. And if your friend does it that way, he's doing it wrong!

Network marketing is—plain and simple—about sharing things you love with people you suspect will love them, too. It's about asking people to consider redirecting the dollars already headed out the door to something they might like better; something that benefits them *and* you.

This is no different from how it works in any other business or community. If your friend owned a restaurant, would you eat there? Would you be offended if they asked you to try a dish? Of course not. If your friend was performing in a concert, would you buy a ticket? We think you would.

Do you recommend your friends for jobs? Set them up on dates? Sponsor them in charity walks, donate to their causes, or loan them a few bucks? Do they "like" your stuff on Facebook, comment on your blog, shop at your store, frequent your salon, and send business your way? Is your freezer full of Girl Scout cookies and fundraiser candy bars? Did you get tax, legal, medical, and business advice last year? *For free?*

Okay then. So why, when a friend asks you to try a sample or browse a catalog, are you suddenly so annoyed?

We're not asking you to eat at our restaurant for breakfast, lunch, and dinner, or see our show *every* night of the week. We're not asking you to *sustain* us; we're asking you to *support* us. Just as we'd support you.

So, if that means we're *using* our friendships, then fine. Guilty as charged.

#8: High Failure Rate

Your friend, your cousin, your colleague, your colleague's cousin's friend—everyone knows someone who's "failed" at network marketing.

We're not here to deny the statistics about the success rate of network marketing. They are what they are. But we do want to warn *you* that while the numbers may not lie, they certainly don't tell the whole story.

So here it is.

Some People Are Not Qualified to Do It

Network marketing may be simple, but it's not always easy. Like any other endeavor worth pursuing—college, graduate school, sports, acting, a military career, etc.—network marketing requires a certain skill set and character. We're talking about ambition, a work ethic, people skills, persistence, patience, a positive attitude, commitment, self-reflection, and the willingness to learn. If a person doesn't have these traits, and isn't willing to acquire them, he or she will *not* succeed at network marketing.

Sadly, most of the people who join network marketing companies *just to get rich quick* don't have these qualities. That's how they ended up doing network marketing to begin with—they weren't *qualified* for anything else. So don't be fooled by the numbers. These people would lower the success rate of any profession; network marketing is just the one that let them in.

Besides, have you ever done the research on just how many people in America have graduate degrees, reach top military positions, own successful businesses after five years, play professional sports, or make more than $100,000 per year? Okay then. The world is full of people who don't have or do what it takes to make it to the top. Network marketing is no different.

People Quit Too Soon

Second, the only way to truly fail in network marketing is to quit. And the majority of people quit way too soon.

Network marketing attracts a lot of folks expecting to become the next rags-to-riches story, and they want to cash in yesterday. So they get involved in the business, discover that it actually takes time and work to make money, and then quit. When they do, they tell the whole world that network marketing doesn't work.

Network marketing *does* work. It just didn't work for them. People who are looking to get something for nothing are common in network marketing. And they're more likely to blame the profession—, rather than their lack of effort or skills—for their failures. They've done it in every aspect of their life—diets, marriages, careers. The list goes on.

Like starting a business, going to college, or entering a challenging profession, it can take months or even years before the investments in network marketing really pay off. That's because, by their nature, networks take time to grow. The progress builds over time, and the most dramatic success occurs at the *end*, not the beginning. The exercise on the next page will help you understand why.

Understanding The Growth Pattern of Network Marketing

The Million Dollar Question: Would you rather have $1 million today, or one penny, doubled each day for thirty days?

The majority of people would rather have $1 million, because they don't understand the concept of exponential growth. As you can see in the adjacent diagram, just like a network marketing business, it takes time for multiplication to yield significant results. In the beginning, the results don't look very impressive. But *the math doesn't lie*. Eventually, the reward becomes substantial.

This is why people who quit network marketing too soon never reap the benefits of their initial efforts. Just like exercise, dieting, saving money... it's doing the small things consistently. Their short-term blindness prevents them from seeing the long-term vision. They feel under-compensated in the beginning, and don't wait to be overcompensated in the end. In network marketing, you can work hard for a *short* time, so that you don't have to work hard for a *long* time.

The Importance of Having Long Term Vision

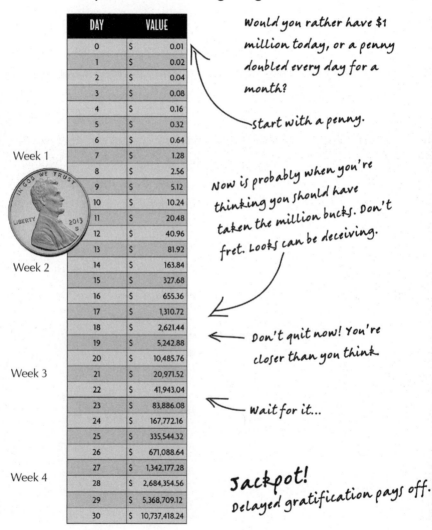

	DAY	VALUE
	0	$ 0.01
	1	$ 0.02
	2	$ 0.04
	3	$ 0.08
	4	$ 0.16
	5	$ 0.32
	6	$ 0.64
Week 1	7	$ 1.28
	8	$ 2.56
	9	$ 5.12
	10	$ 10.24
	11	$ 20.48
	12	$ 40.96
	13	$ 81.92
Week 2	14	$ 163.84
	15	$ 327.68
	16	$ 655.36
	17	$ 1,310.72
	18	$ 2,621.44
	19	$ 5,242.88
	20	$ 10,485.76
Week 3	21	$ 20,971.52
	22	$ 41,943.04
	23	$ 83,886.08
	24	$ 167,772.16
	25	$ 335,544.32
	26	$ 671,088.64
	27	$ 1,342,177.28
Week 4	28	$ 2,684,354.56
	29	$ 5,368,709.12
	30	$ 10,737,418.24

Would you rather have $1 million today, or a penny doubled every day for a month?

→ start with a penny.

Now is probably when you're thinking you should have taken the million bucks. Don't fret. Looks can be deceiving.

← Don't quit now! You're closer than you think.

← Wait for it...

Jackpot!
Delayed gratification pays off.

We know this won't stop people from treating network marketing as a lottery ticket, or feeling cheated when they're still broke after a few weeks. But at the risk of sounding like a broken record, the fact that these people have failed has *nothing to do with you.* Like we said, these are some of the most financially unsuccessful people in the world. They wouldn't recognize delayed gratification if it punched them in the face. They are the same people who think the Lotto is a valid retirement plan and expect Ed McMahon to knock on their door. The fact that they have unrealistic expectations about network marketing, or are the first to buy into obvious hype, isn't out of the ordinary for these people. It's par for the course.

So, yes, there are casualties in network marketing. But there are no victims.

> Most people don't achieve significant financial wealth [in network marketing]. That's because they don't define specific goals and make the necessary commitment of time and energy to achieve them.
>
> Dr. Charles W. King, Author and Professor of Network Marketing

What Constitutes Failure?

The real problem with trying to calculate how many people have failed at network marketing is that there is no agreed-upon definition of failure. There are all different types of stories in network marketing—some that might be classified as failure to one, and success to another.

For example, there are people in network marketing making only meager amounts of money because their networks are new and small. The larger paychecks are in the not-too-distant future. Are *they* failures? There are also people who aren't even in network marketing for the money. They do it for the camaraderie, the community support, the personal development and—above all—the discounts! They're happy right where they are. Are *they* failures? And there are people who decided to give network marketing a whirl, or try their luck to see if they could achieve overnight success. They didn't, and so they quit. Are *they* failures? Or are they just quitters?

What we're saying is, it's obviously impossible to take a snapshot of the network marketing profession and reach any conclusive results about its success rate. And even if you do, what's that got to do with you?

The realistic people know that success in network marketing isn't about chance or luck. It's not about hedging your bets based on what other people have or haven't done. Network marketing is about rolling the dice on *yourself*. So you tell us, are those good odds?

Now we can get to the good stuff: what's so great about network marketing.

CHAPTER FOUR

Get This

> There are those who live in a dream world, and there are some who face reality: and then there are those who turn one into the other.
>
> Douglas H. Everett

Now, obviously we think network marketing is an ingenious concept; otherwise we wouldn't be doing it. But the question isn't whether network marketing is the right or wrong profession. The question is whether it's right for *you*.

So we'll just tell you what we love about it, and you can decide for yourself.

The Top Reasons We Dig This Gig

#1: You Don't Have to Trade Time for Money

Whether you're an employee, freelancer, or small business owner, whether you make $10 an hour or $10,000, the trap is the same. You want the paycheck? You do the time.

Face it, that's how most of us were raised—to believe that we had to earn our living with an "honest day's work." But *let's be honest*: that system is broken. It's an exhausting way to live, and it's not getting easier anytime soon.

Network marketing is entirely different. It's not about trading time for money, or hours in and dollars out. It's about *ongoing income*—income that compounds upon itself—that pays time and time again for an initial phase of work.

Everyone in the world wants continual income. People write books for it, launch companies for it, invent products for it, film movies for it—all in the name of making money while they sleep. But those paths are incredibly difficult, and even riskier to boot. Network marketing is one of the only places where long-term income is a realistic possibility for the *rest of us*.

In network marketing, this continual income grows from three basic steps: (1) learning about the company's offering; (2) spreading the word about it; and (3) teaching other people to do the same. Do this a few times, and before you know it, you're cloned. The people you trained train their own, who in turn do the same. It's a ripple effect that all started by you throwing a stone.

Now *that's* a good trade.

Whether you're feeling sick, or just plain sick of work, you probably don't have a good exit plan—not for tomorrow *or* when you're sixty-five. Well, at least not if you want to live comfortably. But in network marketing, a successful business can run itself without you. Sure, it takes time to get to that point—they don't sprout up overnight—but it's nice to know that eventually you can take a time out (or ten), and the paycheck will never know.

> On the front end [of network marketing], you work very hard and expect nothing in return. On the back end, you're paid far more than you worked for.
>
> Dr. Tom Barrett, Author and Network Marketing Expert

> I walked away from designing my life around my work, into Network Marketing, where life and work can peacefully coexist, free of the constant conflict of having to choose one over the other.
> Why? Because I woke up to the fact that, in my twenty years of being a mom to four amazing children, I'd missed each of their first days of school, field trips, special events, parades, and recitals. Within the first week of new found freedom, I attended my first field trip. The face of my ten year old son as I drove him and his friends, was priceless!
>
> Laura Evans, Network Marketer

#2: Freedom and Flexibility

Work in your pajamas, *check*. Long lunches with friends, check. Run errands mid-day, lose the commute, stay at home with your kids when they're sick—*check, check, check*.

A successful network marketing business allows you to plan your work around your life, instead of your life around your work. Open the calendar, block out the most important things to do, and work *around* them. Your office can be the local coffee shop, a nice resort, a friend's house, or your couch. It's up to you.

Even better, you don't just get to decide where you want to work;

you can decide where you want to *live*. Do you want to be closer to family and friends? Are you tired of the horrible weather where you are? Welcome to the world of choices! Thanks to technology, you can plug into your business from any corner of the globe.

On top of that, network marketing offers you the flexibility to grow your business at your own pace. You can literally fit it into the cracks and crevices of life—a happy hour here, a coffee chat there, a phone call on your way to work. Before you know it, that tiny infant that required so much attention will be a full-grown adult on its own.

> I started my network marketing business with a six-month old, a three-year-old, and a thriving public relations consultancy. Within a year, I had built a six-figure income. In less than three years, I'd earned a million dollars. It's hard work to build that quickly, but it was on my terms, from home, around the kids. The "turn-key" entrepreneurship that network marketing offers is the only way I could have done this.
>
> Romi Neustadt, Network Marketer

#3: A Business in a Box

These days, people want the benefits of owning a business (tax advantages, anyone?) but without the headache.

Network marketing offers just that—no product development, research, manufacturing, hiring, firing, designing, negotiating, managing, shipping, receiving, planning, or billing. No lawyers, accountants, patents, logos, storefronts, or office space. You don't even have to come up with a great idea! Network marketers have the best of both worlds—an infrastructure and proven product or service to plug right into, but without the same risk or expense.

But that's not all. The best part is that network marketing companies have some of the most helpful and comprehensive training around. From product demonstrations and seminars to national conferences and courses on personal growth, you can attend, join, log on, or replay any time you need information and support. In that respect, it's like a business school, but one where the tuition is practically free.

Yeah, we know there's nothing fancy about a business in a box, but sitting on the beach instead of in a cubicle is pretty glamorous, don't you think?

#4: You Get Paid What You're Worth

No time cards, hourly commitments, or staring at the clock. In network marketing, the compensation is simple—you get paid for your *effectiveness*, not your effort. The better you are at what you do, the more you get paid. And the less time you have to spend doing it.

Now, this isn't the part where we tell you that you can become a rock star overnight. This isn't where we promise you millions. But this is where we tell you that the income potential in network marketing is far greater than in most other professions.

It's true. Network marketing isn't about door-to-door sales anymore. It isn't about $20 here and $40 there. The real business of network marketing is about getting paid by the company for your work, and paid well, at that.

Unlike any other job or career, in this business, people who have the exact same title or started at the exact same time can make vastly different amounts of money. There are people who have been in it for years, making less than $25 a month, and people who have been in it for months, replacing six-figure incomes. Some of the highest earners in network marketing have been known to make hundreds of thousands of dollars per month (yes, you read that right—*per month*), and a significant amount of that income is recurring.

Truthfully, the statistics suggest that this won't be most of us. It's estimated that less than 3% of the people in network marketing make that kind of "gangster" money. But a large number of people still make a great living (that either substantially supplements, matches, or exceeds their regular income). So if that sounds good to you, it's important to understand how it all works.

We know what you're thinking: How is it possible that companies can afford to pay such high compensations? Where the heck is that money coming from? *It sounds too good to be true.*

Well, it isn't. And the answer is simple. It comes from cutting out the middlemen—the layers and layers of people and entities that get paid for marketing and distribution. These can typically represent millions of dollars in costs that don't add *any* value to the products themselves.

We realize that sounds abstract to a lot of people, especially if they've never been behind the scenes of a business. So to fully illustrate just how much extra dough network marketing companies are saving by doing this—and how they can issue such large paychecks without breaking the bank—let's look at an example.

Take soda pop for instance: After they're done concocting the recipe, designing the packaging, and manufacturing it, the average beverage company has spent maybe three to ten cents a can—*max*—and even less per ounce if it's headed for fountains.

Now they have to get that soda into your hands—the consumer. They do that through grocery stores, mini-marts, movie theaters, restaurants, vending machines, ballparks, and more. But forming relationships with these places is no easy task.

They have to get their attention, just like they have to get yours. They do *that* through brokers, agents, distributors, and sales reps.

That's not all. Just because the soda is on the shelf doesn't mean you'll buy it. They still have to convince you to choose their brand over the hundreds of others in contention. They do *that* through marketing—agencies, billboards, commercials, direct mail, coupons, magazine spreads, sponsorships, web ads, and spokespeople. As if that weren't enough, they also pay highly-trained publicists to finagle a little "free" press, too.

So let's review—these are all the folks who might have gotten paid for your soda:

- Manufacturer/Factory
- Distributor
- Wholesaler
- Agent
- Broker
- Sales representative
- Ad agency
- Publicist
- Spokesperson
- Media outlets (TV network, magazine, website, billboard owner)

And who paid them? *You* did—fifty cents at the grocery

store, a dollar at the vending machine, a buck-fifty at the fast food joint, three dollars at the theater, and five dollars at the ballpark or concert. Your final price depends on the individual expenses of these entities, the biggest of which is real estate. Yep, that's right—you paid to turn their lights on, too.

Here's a chart to show you the breakdown.

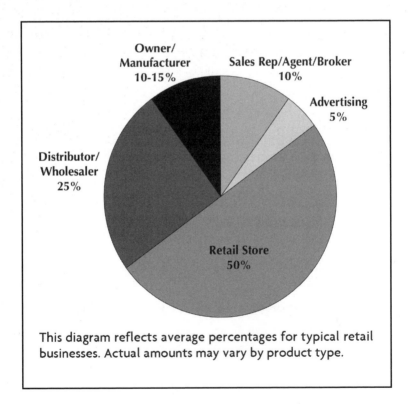

This diagram reflects average percentages for typical retail businesses. Actual amounts may vary by product type.

Feel suckered? You should. The bulk of what you're paying isn't for the product at all. *You're paying to hear about it.*

Now, do you feel inspired to cut some costs for yourself and your friends? Is word-of-mouth marketing starting to make some sense? Good. Let's take a look at the network marketing distribution model on the next page.

See the difference? All that money the company is saving gets passed on to other people—to you, the consumer (so you can get high quality products for a *better* price), and to the network marketer—the person who's actually using it—as opposed to some supermodel on TV.

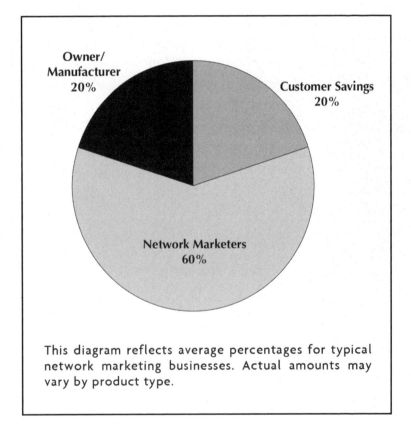

This diagram reflects average percentages for typical network marketing businesses. Actual amounts may vary by product type.

Here it is again!

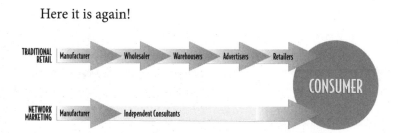

So the next time you hear about some huge network marketing success story and think the whole thing is just hogwash, consider this—it might be *hype* (we can't prevent creeps from misrepresenting incomes), but it might also be *very true*.

Corporations like network marketing because they're paying for advertising that benefits the consumer. If a company like T-Mobile hires Catherine Zeta Jones and pays her $20 million, as charming as she is, that $20 million doesn't benefit the consumer.

In network marketing, the same $20 million goes to distributors who have (hopefully) mastered the product and are able to explain it to the consumer.

Tim Sales, Network Marketing Expert, Author, and Trainer

We could go on and on about what network marketing money has done to transform people's lives, from eliminating debt to funding businesses, hobbies, medical needs, vacations, college educations, cars, homes, and more. It's given people the freedom to play, retire, work less, donate more, and *enjoy* their family and friends. Whatever the case, you get to decide. It's *your* need. It's *your* dream. So it's *your* choice.

We realize that these days, people aren't that great at dreaming. Somewhere along the way, all the visions and fairy tales they had as children got squashed by the real world. Well, it's time to get them back. It's time to flex that imagination muscle and kick it into gear.

So you tell us. What's on your wish list? What could you do with more time and more money?

It seems like everyone has a different answer to this question. For some, it's just a matter of finally getting that pair of designer jeans they've been coveting; for others, it's a closet full of custom haute couture. Some folks just want a brand new piece of furniture, or to fix those nagging repairs around the house. Others are aiming for the entire remodel, or even a second home. Maybe you'd like a little extra cash to be able to eat out whenever you want? Or enough to hire your own personal chef.

Wouldn't it be nice to have the money to visit friends and

loved ones who live far away? Care to fly there First Class? Would you like to spoil your kids on Christmas? Or yourself, your parents, and your friends... *all year long*? What about adopting a family in need for the holidays? Or five? Or even ten? How about donating your money *and* your time to your favorite cause, mission, or cure?

Maybe it's just the ability to pay your bills on time, or spend money on yourself without the guilt. Like we said, it's up to you. You can be practical or you can be lavish. You can save yourself or you can save the world.

Whatever you decide, just remember—network marketing itself doesn't have to be your dream. It doesn't even have to be your passion. But maybe, *just maybe*, it can pay for what is.

> Most people are like I was: they dismiss this opportunity right out of the gate because they don't have an accurate understanding of what is possible, and the kind of income that can be created through the network marketing model. I've found another way to create Major League Baseball money without the risks and headaches of owning a traditional business.
>
> Todd Stottlemyre, former Major League Baseball player and three-time World Champion

#5: You Get to Choose Who You Work With

We're not gonna lie: One of the reasons we like network marketing is because it's like summer camp for adults. You get to meet amazing new people, work with the friends and loved ones you choose, train with the best mentors around, and hang with successful, positive folks whose primary goal is to help YOU. Yes, it's as fun as it sounds.

In network marketing, the camaraderie is built in. You simply can't get rich by yourself. Think about it. The only way for you to reach your goals is by helping other people reach theirs. So you're in business *for* yourself, but never *by* yourself. What's not to love?

Say goodbye to those annoying coworkers, the back-stabbing, tattling, and cut-throat environments. This is a brand new kind of tribe.

#6: You Don't Need a Huge Network to Be Successful

Perhaps the biggest misconception about network marketing is that you have to have a huge network and hundreds of friends to be successful. That couldn't be further from the truth. In fact, you don't even have to have ten friends to be successful. If network marketing were door-to-door sales, the number of clients would matter. But in network marketing, your net*work* is your net *worth*—cheesy, but true. And remember, your "network" will most likely consist of people you didn't originally know.

Allow us to illustrate the beauty of this concept by using an example of something you already do. Let's take your favorite restaurant. You love it, right? So you tell two friends about how much you love it. They each decide to try it, and they love it too. So they tell their friends, who in turn do the same. If this continues, within a few weeks a few dozen people will be eating at the same restaurant (and talking about it, tweeting about it, blogging about it)—all because of *you*.

Now let's assume that you told two more people about that same restaurant, for a total of four, and they each told four, with a similar progression. Now, in the same amount of time, hundreds or even thousands of people—most of whom you've never met—are eating at the same restaurant (and talking about it, tweeting about it, blogging about it)—all because of *you*. Remember, the difference in the beginning was only two people. The difference in the end was *thousands*. That's the power of multiplication.

The Power of Exponential Growth

The difference between each person sharing with 2 people vs. sharing with 4 people.

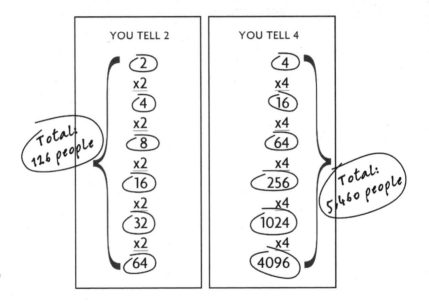

> You can change your whole future… slowly, steadily, and deliberately… by doing something that you've been doing all of your life without realizing it—making referrals.
>
> Nancy Failla, Network Marketing Author and Trainer

You didn't have to quit your job to do this, or talk to hundreds of people. Neither did your friends. This is just how word-of-mouth works. With a few initial connections, you can have *exponential* results.

Obviously, these diagrams reflect exact duplication. The real world of network marketing doesn't look this perfect (it varies as much as the people who do it). Yet the potential is there. And in some cases, it's even greater than this. The numbers are entirely up to you and your team.

As you can see, this isn't a get-rich-quick scheme (although in most cases it's a get-rich-quicker-than-getting-a-Ph.D.-scheme). This is a legitimate business opportunity that takes time and energy to build. *We can't emphasize that enough.* But once the foundation is laid, it's a business that will pay dividends in perpetuity.

Now pay attention. As you can clearly see, you didn't have to be a great salesperson to have success with this system. You weren't a sales rep for the restaurant; you were just a customer who became a loyal fan.

Network marketing is no different. It's about selecting a company you can authentically promote, finding a handful of customers to share it with (you can even be your own customer) and building an organization of people who do the same, one small layer at a time. To do that, you don't need good *salesmanship*; you need good systems, strategy, and leadership.

The best network marketers are people who learn to teach, help, mentor, and empower other people. Not a *ton* of other people; just *some* other people. Okay?

So, if your network is small or you're not a salesperson, come on in. If you don't like helping people, *adiós*.

> The genius part of network marketing is that you don't need to know a lot of people. you just need to know a few who know a few who know a few. The comp plans vary, depending upon the company, but in general, you can build a substantial organization with as few as four leaders.
>
> Iain Pritchard, Network Marketer

#7: Turn an Expense into Income

Yes, you read that right—turn something that costs you money into something that *makes* you money. We know, we know—how is that possible? Well, when you redirect your spending to your own company, you're getting paid to give yourself business. Makes sense, right? If you owned Coke, would you buy a Pepsi? Probably not.

Also, like we said, network marketing products are generally higher in quality than their retail counterparts, which can result in even greater value. And some companies offer their independent consultants the perk of added discounts as well.

Even better, there are usually tax advantages of owning and operating a home-based business. For some people—especially those in traditional employment—the tax benefits can be a huge and welcome relief. Of course, we suggest you check with your tax professional about this.

So whether you want to save money or make money, the choice is yours. Network marketing lets you play both sides of your coins.

#8: Make a Difference with Your Dollars

You hear it all the time—shop local, support your mom-and-pop store, be loyal to the little guy.

It's all the same thing—keep the money close to home. Help your family, your friends, your neighbor, your community. Do it with the purchases you already plan to make.

We're not saying that network marketing companies are the equivalent of the corner store; they're clearly far larger than that. What we're saying is that they work with a lot of independent representatives who are. These people are no different from any other small business owner in your town. Their taxes and profit will be put back into your school systems, parks, businesses, housing market, and municipal programs. They're some of the best investments you can make.

Whether it's the single mom next door, the friend who got downsized, or the struggling family trying to save their home, network marketing is someone's livelihood—someone connected to *you*.

So, the next time you consider buying a bar of soap, a vitamin, or a specialty item from a giant chain, please consider the source.

#9: Take Charge of Your Financial Future

For many of us, the fate of our future is in someone else's hands. Day in and out, many of us sit around waiting for the other shoe to drop—to be told that we're no longer of use.

Network marketing allows you take back the control. You decide *how* to grow your business, how big to grow your business, *where* to grow your business, and *when*. You're not confined to someone else's list, location, rules, or constraints. The only limits are the ones you set.

In this day and age, it can be frightening to feel like your financial bottom line is a matter of fate. With network marketing, whether you do it alongside your job or instead of it, it's just nice to know that when your family needs more bacon, you can bring it home.

#10: The Network Marketing Profession Is Poised to Explode

Network marketing is here to stay. But that doesn't mean it will stay the same. On the contrary, all signs suggest that network marketing is about to embark on one of its largest growth spurts yet, and that means higher numbers in everyone's bottom line.

The Economic Outlook

Like we said, in this uncertain economic climate, people are looking for a back-up plan—a way to supplement (or even replace) their income with something that doesn't eclipse their full-time work. The problem is that many of the options are horrendous. And if you think getting a higher degree is the answer, think again. The U.S. is drowning in $1.3 trillion in student loan debt. That's more than credit card debt and car loans. Does anyone else think that's a little scary? Getting a second job requires a lot more time. Starting a traditional business requires a lot *more time and money*. Network marketing, on the other hand, requires only a little of both.

Whether it's an extra $300 to chip away at some debt, $2,000 to really get ahead, or the goal of turning a Plan B into a Plan A, in network marketing the choice is yours. The amount you make is directly proportional to what you put in. Now *that's* security.

Because of this, people from all walks of life will continue to explore network marketing on their lunch hours and weekends. As a result, network marketers will be in the right place at the right time.

The Rise of Professionalism in Network Marketing

Network marketing certainly has a reputation for welcoming the otherwise unemployable people of the world. And so long as sign-up fees are low, and the income potential remains as great as it is, that won't change.

What *will* change over time is the increase in professional and formally educated people joining network marketing companies.

Even before white collar workers were getting laid off by the thousands, they were turning to network marketing. There are a few reasons for that. First, the idea of getting paid what you're worth—as opposed to some set salary—is incredibly alluring for talented people. Many of these executives had great jobs but were tired of their efforts outshining their paychecks.

Second, the profession itself has been changing—specifically in ways that are attractive to professional people. According to Tom Barrett, author of *Dare to Dream, Work to Win*: "Network marketing has reached new levels of integrity, professionalism, mainstream acceptability, levels of profitability, technological sophistication, training, and support."

Pep rallies and rah-rah conventions have been replaced with online product demonstrations, business opportunity meetings, conference calls, and video presentations. These transformations are legitimizing the profession for people who wouldn't otherwise give it the time of day.

For those who have what it takes to be successful in other areas of their life, network marketing is a hotbed of opportunity. We're not saying it's Easy Street; we're just saying that for folks with some drive, intelligence, and a work ethic, network marketing is one of the simplest ways to earn a living. And accomplished professionals are starting to figure that out. Every week, another 175,000 Americans join a network marketing company.

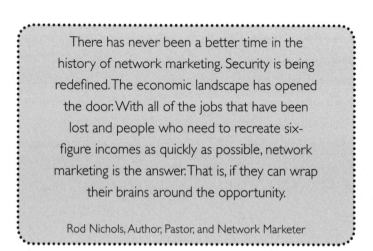

There has never been a better time in the history of network marketing. Security is being redefined. The economic landscape has opened the door. With all of the jobs that have been lost and people who need to recreate six-figure incomes as quickly as possible, network marketing is the answer. That is, if they can wrap their brains around the opportunity.

Rod Nichols, Author, Pastor, and Network Marketer

Going Global

Network marketing isn't just popular in the United States. It's really gaining some ground in the rest of the world as well. In addition to those joining each week in the U.S., 300,000 more are enrolling around the world. That's almost 500,000 new network marketers a week worldwide, and fifty-eight countries participate in The World Federation of The Direct Selling Association. Although the United States has the highest volume of sales from network marketing companies, enormous increases in other countries—some as high as 121% in a five-year period—have been recorded around the world.

Network marketing doesn't have quite the same stigma in other countries it has in the United States, but the economies overseas are still just as fragile. According to World Employment and Social Outlook Trends – 2016, in emerging and developing economies, the number of jobless is expected to rise by 4.8 million over the next two years. The bigger network marketing companies know this, and have already made their move.

As the opportunity for this profession continues to expand overseas, network marketers will be uniquely poised to blitz right through it.

#11: Recognition for a Job Well Done

Other than a holiday card and some fruitcake, when's the last time you were thanked...*just for doing your job*? Have you ever gotten flowers on your birthday...*from your boss*? When you have an idea, suggestion, or concern to register with your company, are you heard...*by the CEO*? Did the last sentence just make you laugh?

It may sound funny, but it's really quite sad. These days, the average employee is no more than the hired help, working longer and harder than ever before. We know the paycheck is great, but let's face it: you're **human**. You want to feel appreciated. We do, too.

In network marketing, you don't just get paid, you *get recognized*. We're not talking about free trips and prizes, or jewelry and fancy cars (although you get those too). We're talking about *real* acknowledgement—a personal call from the president, a private line to customer service, the chance to participate in company decisions, and a "thank you" for a job well done.

When you join a network marketing company, you're not just part of a team; you're a member of a family. Your voice is heard. Your suggestions matter. Your vote is counted. When you meet your numbers, you are *called up* to the stage, *called out* in front of

your peers; you are applauded, praised, celebrated. You are loved.
   Any takers?

Get the Facts

- In 2016, nearly a quarter (24.8 percent) of Americans have less than $100 to their name. Meanwhile, 38 percent said they would pay less than their full credit card balance this month, and 11 percent said they would make the minimum payment—meaning they would likely be mired in debt for years and pay more in interest than they originally borrowed. [vi]

- 63% of Americans don't have enough cash on hand to handle a $500 emergency expense, according to a survey by the National Foundation for Credit Counseling. [vii]

- Numbers of bankruptcies: 1.17 million in 2013, 1.04 million in 2014, and 911,068 in 2015. [viii]

- Approximately 1.1 million jobs in corporate finance, information technology and other business functions were lost at large American and European companies in 2008 and 2009, due to a combination of offshoring, productivity improvements, and lack of economic growth. [ix]

- Unemployment for the U.S. was 4.7% in May 2016. [xi]

- Total outstanding consumer debt has reached $3.4 trillion. [xi]

CHAPTER FIVE

Get Real

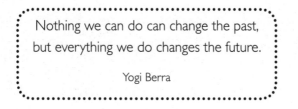

Nothing we can do can change the past,
but everything we do changes the future.

Yogi Berra

Okay, friends. Buckle up. It's time to get serious about our current situation. Housing markets can crash. Job security is obsolete. Social security is in the toilet, and we're almost better off investing in our mattresses than the stock market.

That's right, folks—the name of the game has changed. So we need to stop playing by the same old rules.

It's time to get our heads out of the sand. It's time to face some facts.

First, most people are broke. No matter how much money they make, it's gone at the end of the month. And with multiple credit cards, an upside-down home, and some high-priced student loans, their debt is spiraling out of control. At the rate they're going, the only career that could possibly wipe it out is either illegal or involves some form of nudity. Meanwhile, financial advisors are telling us that our daily Starbucks habit is the cause of our money woes. *Give us a break.* Lattes are not the problem, people. Our *jobs* are.

Hey, you with the golden handcuffs. We're talking to you, too!

You're dreadfully unhappy at work, and the rest of us are miserable just hearing about it. You sulk on Sunday nights like a toddler, and treat Fridays like you've been released from jail. You spend 80% of your week waiting for 20% of it to roll around, and when it does, you're so tired from all the prep work, commuting, and errands that you have no energy to enjoy it. On top of that, you play endless tag-team with your babysitters and then wonder why your kids are so unglued.

You're trading time for money, marching to work every day like a rat in the race to make a buck. You have no backup plan— nothing to sustain you in case of an emergency, disability, illness, or family crisis. Every morning is Groundhog Day, with you dressed in a *different* version of the *same* suit, hoping this year you might get a better desk, office, title, or paycheck. You never do. And when you're disappointed with your job, you run out to find another one *just like it*.

And you're making fun of *network marketing*?

We know, we know—everyone says, "You're so lucky just to be employed." *No, you're not*! Don't sell yourself short! You're not *lucky* to be working 60-hour weeks for 40-hour pay, or wondering from day to day whether you'll be employed this time next year. You are not *blessed* to wake up to an alarm clock and beg for unpaid leave. You weren't *spared* when you were demoted, downsized, furloughed, and deprived of all your benefits instead of losing your job.

When did *that* become good fortune?

Have you taken a look around lately? Your retirement fund has vanished. Social security is everything *but* secure, and at the rate our country is going, you won't be able to retire until you're dead. If you happen to make it before then, statistics suggest you'll be living on less than half the income you had before. So it might be time to lose those visions of climbing the Great Wall of China and boating down a Venice canal. *Not gonna happen.*

By the way, how is your health? Are you happy with the way you feel? Are you tired of getting six hours of sleep at night and hitting the snooze button with the force of a missile? Does it take three cups of coffee just to do your job? Are you comfy there, eating at your desk? Are you happy with the way you look, other than on paper?

Hey, we know that some of you love your jobs, and are even satisfied with the money you make. We're genuinely happy for you. But this is not about whether you like your career or your bank account. This is about whether you like your *life*.

It's time to launch a backup plan before your boss does it for you. It's time to create some space and freedom to really enjoy your days. It's time to stop subscribing to the mob mentality that this is the best that you can do.

Trust us, it's not.

Hey, business owners! Have a seat. We need to chat.

So you did it—you finally gave your boss the finger and struck out on your own. *High five*! You're an artist, an author, an expert, an inventor, an *entrepreneur* (isn't that a neat word?). You're the rebel of your family and the envy of your friends. You relish your newfound freedom and boss-less life. You don't miss those office politics and stuffy corporate meetings. You have jeans to wear and lunches to write off! Never mind that you work 16-hour days and forget to shower. You love what you do! You could do it all day—hunkering down in your dungeon of creativity, with your dreams, charts, graphs, and vision boards of just how you'll *hit it big.*

Good for *you.*

Or maybe you're not trying to win the startup jackpot and instead you just want to be your own boss. Maybe you're a professional—a doctor, a lawyer, a dentist, or an accountant. No buyouts or huge mergers in your future—just plain old freedom and your name on the door. Feels good, doesn't it?

We all agree that this world couldn't survive without the innovation, drive, and imagination of people like you. It's the foundation of our country, the beauty of the human race, and the basis for almost *all* progress. So, our hats off to you, business owners! We dig you.

But we definitely don't envy you.

Let's be honest. That tax write-off isn't so great when you have no income to protect. Family vacations are no fun when your laptop comes along. Going to sleep whenever you want is not so easy when the weight of the world comes with you. Sure, you don't miss a soccer game or recital; you're just on the Blackberry while you're there. You know it's true. Your stack of paperwork is taller than your kid. Your inbox is flooded with nonsense you have no time to read. And just how did so many government agencies find out where you live?

How 'bout those employees, huh? Who knew they could be this much work? They're so darn pushy with their ergonomic needs and payroll demands. Don't they know you have no time for employee handbooks and sexual harassment training? You have a business to run! There's real estate to lease, a website to build, insurance to buy, contracts to write, taxes to pay, logos to make, flyers to print, vendors to meet, clients to please, papers to file, *files* to file, licenses, registrations, and trash to take out (remember when you used to have a janitor?). Can't you get a *break*?

And just between you and us, are you lonely? We know how it is. You don't miss those annoying co-workers, but it would be fun to have a little water cooler chit-chat now and then, right? Let's face it: Isolation is tough. But the idea of another networking function makes you want to gag.

Look, we hate to state the obvious—especially because we know how much you love the title of *Founder*—but unless you can walk away tomorrow and survive, it looks like all you *found* was another job.

We get that network marketing just doesn't compare to owning your own gig. It's not creative, industrious, or bold. It's not...*original*.

We agree. It's just not the same. But in case you haven't noticed, we're trying to earn a living, not a Nobel Peace Prize. We want to stay at home with our kids as much as you do. We want to wear our flip-flops to meetings, too. We want money for our hobbies, our passions, our recreation, and our futures—*just like you*.

So now that you know how great the opportunity is in network marketing, especially compared to the low risk, we have just one question: What kind of an entrepreneur would you be if you passed it up?

Wait! We're not done yet. Stay-at-home moms, drop that sippy cup and come over here for a sec.

You are the *true* heroes—the ones fighting the battle on the front lines. You take on the meanest of ear infections, the largest of laundry stacks, the loudest of temper tantrums, and the dirtiest of diapers, dishes, counters, and fingers. You are everything to everyone—cook, maid, wife, mom, assistant, peacekeeper, and CEO. True, it's the hardest job of your life, but you've got it all under control. And you wouldn't even think about going back to that corner office with those rock-star benefits, because you have the best title of all: *Mom*.

Sure, you're starved for some adult conversation, and even make unnecessary grocery store runs just to engage the clerk. Yeah, you'd give your right arm for eight consecutive hours of sleep. Oh, who are we kidding? Six. And so what if *Mickey Mouse Clubhouse* on replay is starting to feel like a form of medieval water torture? You wouldn't trade this for the world!

We get it. The luxury of being able to stay at home with your kids is one of life's greatest gifts. But let's get real. Wouldn't you like to have some more dough? Just a little slush-fund so you could stop hearing so much about that nasty "B" word—*budget*? Admit it—you miss those designer jeans and mani-pedis, or that buttery leather tote you traded for the enormous diaper bag. That fuller than full-time job would look a heck of a lot better after a massage or two, right? It's OK, you can tell us.

Wouldn't it be nice to have a little creativity, fun, and camaraderie back in your life? Or an excuse to get out of the house so you can hang with your friends? Wouldn't controlling the purse strings be a lot more fun when *your* money is in it?

Don't be afraid to fess up—you want a little somethin'-somethin' of your own. It's not selfish; it's *normal*.

We know network marketing won't give you that fancy job back or an expense account that doesn't quit; but if you dust off those talents of yours, it just *might* give you the perks that came with 'em.

So tell your man to take that budget and shove it, sister. Let's roll.

Baby Boomers! Grab your bifocals—this part is for you.

You've put in the work and you've done the time. Now bring on the next chapter of life, right? We know that you're ready for it; we can tell you've got plans. You have hobbies to learn, lessons to take, boats to sail, and golf clubs to buy. And wouldn't that spare bedroom look nice as a gym?

Go for it. Who's going to stop you? Certainly not us.

You deserve it—your nest is empty, your dues are paid. So break out those travel guides, and chill that champagne! Life has just begun!

Or so you thought.

Actually, this time isn't what you thought it would be, is it? The second you got an empty nest, you got an empty retirement fund, too. What happened to all that money? Wasn't that investment supposed to be "low-risk" How will you get that income back?

Where do you go from here?

All of a sudden, the world is upside-down. Computer whiz kids are getting jobs that people with forty years of experience deserve. Employees with decades of loyalty under their belts are getting laid off. And just when you thought you were done taking care of other people, you find yourself juggling more needs than ever before. You've got aging parents to shuttle to doctor's appointments, grown kids who need financial help, and grandkids you want to spend more time with. You're stuck in a generation sandwich, caught between your bills, their bills, walkers, car seats, and more.

So much for a life of leisure.

Well, in case you haven't caught on, we have a solution—one that allows you to re-secure your financial future and give you the freedom and flexibility to finally relax. Not only that, it gives you the chance to expand your circle, make new friends, get re-energized, and feel useful and valuable again.

With network marketing, the job description is simple: *Friendly company seeks enthusiastic individuals who love helping people and are willing to learn. Life experience a plus. Work wherever and whenever you want.*

So, what do you say? Think you fit the bill?

Listen, we realize that it's not fun to be scared of retirement, or to have to think about your money all over again. We know that in this day and age, you might not be able to get the job or the income you so clearly deserve. But cheer up, friends. With network marketing, you might be able to find something better—*and a lot more fun.*

Get the Facts

- According to a Right Management survey, 88% of U.S. workers said they were either somewhat or totally unsatisfied with their jobs. [xii]

- Depression rates are ten times higher today than they were in 1960, and every year the age threshold of unhappiness sinks lower. [xiii]

- The 40-hour workweek was originally designed to give Americans more time and more freedom. The Fair Labor Standards Act (29 U.S. Code Chapter 8), as first proposed under the New Deal, was one of the first pieces of legislation to reduce the workweek for certain industries to a maximum of 44 hours (down from 50, and before that, 60). [xi]

- As of 2016, student loan debt totaled almost $1.3 trillion. [xiv] Auto loan debt totaled $1.1 trillion, [xv] and credit card debt totaled $929 billion. [xvi]

- As of 2015, student loans in repayment totaled $397.1 billion, loans in deferment totaled $99.2 billion, loans in forbearance totaled $89.5 billion, and loans in default totaled $50.8 billion. [xvii]

- According to the Department of Commerce, more than 1 million people start traditional businesses each year. 40% of them fail within the first year. Of the remaining businesses, 80% fail within the next five years. Of those, another 80% fail within the subsequent five years. [xviii]

- According to The Wall Street Journal, banks—under scrutiny by regulators—are continuing to strengthen capital reserves, making it difficult even for entrepreneurs with track records and years of experience to qualify for business loans. [xix]

- In the fourth quarter of 2015, venture capitalists invested $11.3 billion, down 32 percent. This quarter marked the eighth consecutive quarter where more than $10 billion was invested in a single quarter, but it also represented the smallest amount invested since the third quarter of 2014. [xx]

CHAPTER SIX

Get a Plan

> The best way to predict the
> future is to create it.
>
> Abraham Lincoln

It's time to get real about your money, honey.

So far, you've figured out that it doesn't grow on trees. That's good. But have you noticed lately that it also doesn't grow in the stock market or in bank accounts?

Unfortunately, your house is no breadwinner, either. It went from being an asset to a liability overnight. Sort of like a credit card with a roof and a yard.

If you think your job is an investment, think again. The average wages for the middle class haven't gone up in ten years. And unless you consider a gold watch and pat on the back to be a good return on a 35-year investment, it's a loser. Besides, when you switch companies, you're back at square one.

Now let's talk about your savings account. First, congrats on even having one! In this economy, you are a rare breed. But what will it be worth a few years from now, when inflation skyrockets, but your balance doesn't? What can a savings account really do for you anyway, aside from offer a few bucks in the case of an emergency or retail splurge? And what will you do after it gets wiped out?

Seriously, what happens when you don't want to work anymore? Or worse, *can't* work anymore? What if you or your spouse gets laid off? What will you do when a family member needs your help? Or you want another baby, a new car, home, wedding, or college fund? What are your options for creating additional or passive income?

As you can see from the diagram on the following page, you don't really have many.

First, whether it's a CD, Money Market Account, or savings account, you have to *have* money to make money. At the current interest rates, to make an extra $200 a month in passive income, you'd have to have more than $120,000 sitting in the bank as we speak. That's right—*sitting*.

This chart reflects how much income is created from a traditional savings account.

To earn $200 per month	
Interest Rate	Amount in the Bank
2%	$120,000.00
3%	$80,000.00
4%	$60,000.00
5%	$48,000.00
6%	$40,000.00
7%	$34,286.00
8%	$30,000.00
9%	$26,666.80
10%	$24,000.00

To earn $500 per month	
Interest Rate	Amount in the Bank
2%	$362,000.00
3%	$240,000.00
4%	$180,000.00
5%	$144,000.00
6%	$120,000.00
7%	$102,857.00
8%	$90,000.00
9%	$80,001.00
10%	$72,000.00

To earn $800 per month	
Interest Rate	Amount in the Bank
2%	$480,000.00
3%	$320,000.00
4%	$240,000.00
5%	$192,000.00
6%	$160,000.00
7%	$137,143.00
8%	$120,000.00
9%	$106,667.00
10%	$96,000.00

To earn $1,000 per month	
Interest Rate	Amount in the Bank
2%	$600,000.00
3%	$400,000.00
4%	$300,000.00
5%	$240,000.00
6%	$200,000.00
7%	$171,429.00
8%	$150,000.00
9%	$133,335.00
10%	$120,000.00

To earn $5,000 per month	
Interest Rate	Amount in the Bank
2%	$3,000,000.00
3%	$2,000,000.00
4%	$1,500,000.00
5%	$1,200,000.00
6%	$1,000,000.00
7%	$857,143.00
8%	$750,000.00
9%	$666,668.00
10%	$600,000.00

To earn $10,000 per month	
Interest Rate	Amount in the Bank
2%	$6,000,000.00
3%	$4,000,000.00
4%	$3,000,000.00
5%	$2,400,000.00
6%	$2,000,000.00
7%	$1,714,285.00
8%	$1,500,000.00
9%	$1,333,335.00
10%	$1,200,000.00

So how much money do you have in YOUR savings account?

Even if the interest rates improve to 5% in the near future, you'd still have to have $48,000 *available* to invest—all to receive that same $200 a month.

Most of us don't have that kind of money sitting around. And even if we did, it wouldn't be worth it to plop it in some account that moves like a snail. You'd have to get started at the age of twenty for it to be worth it by the time you're sixty-five.

So what's the answer? Something with a little more risk and a lot more reward? The stock market, maybe?

That *might* have been the answer in 1985, but as a lot of broke Baby Boomers will tell you today, ten years ago they would have been better off putting their money into high stakes poker than the NASDAQ. Since the Great Depression, the stock market has crashed three times. Two of those times were in the last ten years.

Now do you think network marketing looks silly?

Listen, we think it's great that some of you have no debt, and that you've managed to put a few pennies away for a rainy day. But you shouldn't have any illusions about just how far that will get you—in this economy or at *all*.

Nowhere else is there a lower investment with a higher rate of return than in network marketing. For less than a few hundred bucks, you get the chance to earn $200 a month, $1,000 a month, $10,000 a month and more, in far less time. And unlike almost every other opportunity around, you don't have to put yourself into debt first, spending twenty years of your life paying back your loans one cent at a time—all before you have enough to invest.

Are you catching on?

Day in and out, we hear from smug friends who inquire about how our network marketing businesses are doing after ten or twelve weeks. *Puh-lease.* What were your stocks making after ninety days in the market? How much interest was in your savings account after the first few months? Were you rolling in the dough after three months at your entry-level job?

Wake up, folks. It's time to take a critical look at why certain things in our society are respected and others are rejected.

Yes, we know that in network marketing there's *no* guarantee. But unlike a lot of other options covered here, the outcome is largely within your control. So before you go throwing your money at the next broker or banker you see, consider putting it into the wisest investment of all—*you.*

Get the Facts

- According to an article in *Business Week*, as Baby Boomers age, there will be more retirees collecting benefits and fewer workers paying taxes. The current Social Security program is fiscally sound until 2041, at which time it will cover 80% of promised benefits. [xxi]

- When Social Security was adopted in the United States in 1935, the retirement age was set at 65, but life expectancy was 62.5 years. The average person died before they could collect. [xxii]

- As of July 2010, both Republican and Democratic leaders of the House of Representatives indicated that the retirement age will likely be raised to 70 over the next few years, a change that will impact the Social Security benefits of all people ages 50 and younger. [xxiii]

- A recent report by AARP finds that nearly half of Americans 50 and over have $25,000 or less saved for retirement. [xxiv]

CHAPTER SEVEN

Get Involved

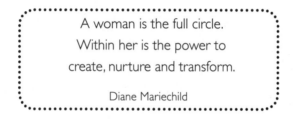

> A woman is the full circle.
> Within her is the power to
> create, nurture and transform.
>
> Diane Mariechild

It's a level playing field, ladies. So get in the game.

That's right. Network marketing is one of the only places where women have none of the limitations of mainstream society. No barriers, boys' clubs, glass ceilings, or salary gaps. No full-time hours, hellish commutes, or skimpy maternity leave. It's one of the most equitable compensation options around.

But that's not the only reason women outnumber men in this business by four to one. Here are a few more.

It's Second Nature

Like we said, the opportunity in network marketing is equal

on paper, but in reality, we women actually have a gigantic genetic edge. It's a business where many of our greatest strengths—socializing, connecting, nurturing, teaching, and relating—*are part of the job*. It's a place where sharing, talking, togetherness, camaraderie, and teamwork enhance the bottom line.

Now *that's* what we call a learning curve.

Don't get us wrong. It's not like we sit around all day singing songs and braiding each other's hair.

Network marketing can really be hard work at times—facing rejection, battling the stigma, and working with diverse personality types. But it is a place where we can be who we are and instantly be good at what we do. Imagine that. You haven't even started and already you're a natural!

Women are also attracted to the sense of community that comes from network marketing. Men may tease us about the fact that we go to the ladies' room together, but it's true—we like to travel in packs. Network marketing gives us the chance to do that, but in a financially productive way.

In this business, individual success equals group success, and competition is to our *dis*advantage. Sure we might be stereotyped as catty by some, but we know the truth. Women want to triumph *together*. Now we can.

Women Need This Now More Than Ever

It's the 21st century. We fought, we picketed, we protested, we won. Now here we are, standing on the shoulders of our female ancestors, and you know what? The view's not so great.

Sure, we can conquer Corporate America *and* still rule the roost. We can bring home the bacon *and* fry it up! We have choices! *Tons and tons of choices...*

But for some reason, we're still stuck. We know we can have it all. We're just not sure how to manage it all.

Many of us are putting off having kids because we're afraid that having a baby means losing a career. Then we're faced with the hazard of bearing children later in life. Or planning it in the sweet spot—where neither professional success nor biological clock is a threat. Some of us are delaying marriage, figuring that our chances for career growth, travel, and independence might be compromised if we don't. Then we end up dealing with the pitfalls of being single, and alone, in a dual-income world.

Others are settling down, building homes, and having families, only to realize that we worked all those years to get so educated, so qualified, so experienced—for what? And still some of us are doing it all—holding down the fort and the job—maybe because we want to, or maybe because we have to. Either way, we can barely breathe.

We're not saying that network marketing is the only way to have your cake and eat it too. We're just saying that as far as balancing, juggling, managing, and *savoring* each slice, it's about the best option we've ever seen.

> Don't be trapped by dogma—which is living with the results of other people's thinking. Don't let the noise of others' opinions drown out your own inner voice. And, most important, have the courage to follow your heart and intuition. They somehow already know what you truly want to become. Everything else is secondary.
>
> Steve Jobs, Co-Founder, Chairman, and CEO of Apple Inc.

Women Want to Make a Difference

We love our independence, but what we really want is *influence*.

For women, the ability to effect change and make an impact is paramount. We don't just want to better ourselves. We want to better our children, our schools, our communities, and our planet.

According to the U.S. Bureau of Labor Statistics, 62 million

Americans engaged in volunteer work at least once between September 2014 and September 2015. And women outnumbered men in that regard. Nearly 28% of women volunteered, while only 21.8% of men volunteered. [xxv]

So what's the answer to saving the world? That's easy—give women more time and money!

That sounds great on paper, but the reality is that we're not likely to have either anytime soon. Without a Sugar Daddy or some unexpected windfall, most women are not in the position to move out of financial stability and into dramatic wealth. In 2016, twenty-one Fortune 500 companies were run by women. Though this marks a new high for female CEOs, women still run just 4.2% of Fortune 500 companies. And one in ten Fortune 500 corporations have no women on their boards, according to research by Catalyst. [xxvi] Sure, we're gaining on our male counterparts when it comes to equal opportunities, but we're still limited as far as our ability to take *advantage* of them.

For most of us, basic survival is a day-to-day chore. Our schedule is consumed with getting money in the door, food on the table, and our kids shuttled to and from play dates, activities, and doctor appointments. Any extra time we have is spent engaging in pure luxury, also known as shuttling ourselves to the rare play date, activity, or doctor appointment.

And until we can do more than just keep our heads above water, our chances of having enough time or money for global influence are limited.

Network marketing changes those odds. By offering women a shot at creating substantial ongoing income just by doing what comes naturally, network marketing provides the time *and* money for us to give back to society and leave our mark.

Look, we're not saying that women can't save the world one *hour* or *dollar* at a time. We're just saying that it would be easier with a lot more of both.

Speaking of making a difference, wouldn't it be nice to make a permanent difference in the life of someone you love? Well, now you can. Network marketing gives you the ability to empower your friends and family with the tools to improve their situation *themselves*. We're not talking about a handout; we're talking about a hand *up*.

Everybody has strengths. Everyone has talents, knowledge, and a unique skill-set all their own. Some people love socializing and are naturals at public speaking, teaching, and training, while others have a talent for writing, are great at following up, and are masters at managing the details. Whatever the case, network marketing gives you the chance to reach out to someone in your life—someone who might not have the specific strengths they need to achieve their goals alone—and say, "Hey, let's do this together."

Now you can do more than just *listen* to your friends' problems; you can help solve them. *That's* a big difference to make.

Okay, we can't get out of this chapter without talking about wealth and your relationship to it. Not to get all self-helpy on you, but what's your relationship with abundance? Do you believe that you are allowed to have an abundance of time, freedom, and money?

Are you resistant to having *riches*? Does the word "riches" turn you off? Do you think that fancy cars, jets, and luxury travel are for the boys? If you see a woman enjoying these things, do you assume she married into them?

Most women have an image in their mind of the independently wealthy woman—she's greedy, pushy, selfish, and masculine. She wears power suits and plays poker with the guys. And above all, she's heartless.

But is that true?

What if we told you that the wealthy women we know are fun, fearless, kind, compassionate, philanthropic, free, and *feminine*? Does that change your impression of money? Does it alter your perception of your right to own it?

Making money and having abundance is your natural born right. So when did you associate it with men? Or negativity and greed? How old were you when you were told that money was evil? Or that you should feel guilty for wanting it? When did you decide that being poor was honorable?

Well, it's time for some reprogramming.

Having money is not about being materialistic or judging others for what they don't have. And it's not the most important thing in life. But you know what? It can pay for what is. Whether that's a roof over your head, health insurance, medical bills, your child's college education, a way to quit your job, the ability to fund an orphanage in Africa, or provide clean water for the world, the freedom to choose is yours. And money pays for that freedom.

We don't want you to be impressed with the living we've earned; we want you to feel empowered by it. Empowered to stop settling for less and start expecting more. Empowered to get over your money baggage and silence that inner guilt. Empowered to get out there and *claim your piece of the pie*. It's yours. Go get it. And then—*share it*.

Besides, whoever said that money can't buy happiness is obviously still cleaning her own house.

Get the Facts

- In 2016, women earned 79 cents for every $1 earned by men. [xxvi]

- As of 2016, women are expected to live an average of five to seven years longer than men. [xxvii]

- As of 2015, of the elderly living in poverty, women are twice as likely to live in poverty. [xxviii]

- Single women are some of the poorest in the world. More than 80% of single-parent households in the United States are headed by mothers. 80% of single mothers are employed, of which 50% are full-time workers and 30% are part time. [xxix]

- In 2014, 45% of single mothers lived in poverty with their children. This is up from 27% in 2011. [xxx]

- On average, women spend 17 years of their lives caring for children and 18 years assisting aged parents. [xxi]

CHAPTER EIGHT

Get Over It

> If you're ever going to doubt something,
> doubt your limits.
>
> Don Ward

We'll be the first to admit it: Not everyone is a fit for network marketing. For example, if you're married to your title, your corner office, or your image, *don't* do network marketing. If your favorite part of the high school reunion is handing out your business cards, *don't* do network marketing. If you regularly make public service announcements about how important your job is, *don't* do network marketing. If you love a corporation or entity that doesn't love you back, *don't* do network marketing. If you need instant gratification, are paralyzed by rejection, or require the approval of people you've never met, *don't* do network marketing. If you've gotten through this book and are still skeptical of network marketing, it obviously isn't for you. So, please, *don't* do network marketing.

Seriously though, just because network marketing carries the promise of a gigantic payoff doesn't mean it's without its trials or tribulations. You'd be hard-pressed to find one success story that doesn't come with its own distinct rocky road.

But that's not just the price of network marketing; that's the price of *life*. Either you're in the game or you're not. And if you're in it, there's a chance you'll get bumped, bruised, pushed, and shoved. If you can't take it, go back to the bleachers.

It's completely cliché, but if you want something you've never had, you must do something you've never done. That means moving outside your comfort zone.

We know. You like your comfort zone. It's *comfortable*. But you know what else is comfortable? Your recliner. And a bowl of mac 'n' cheese. But that doesn't mean either is good for your "bottom line." If you want real comfort—*lifelong comfort*—you have to be prepared for a little discomfort and personal growth in the present moment. Whether it's starting a new diet, workout program, or heading off to get a four-year degree, the rules are the same: Delayed gratification is just that—*delayed*. Get used to it.

And so what if network marketing comes with a little rejection? You've never been rejected before? You've never been turned down for a job or a date? You got accepted to every school to which you applied? Okay then. Get over it, and move on.

Speaking of moving on, it might be time to move along from something else too—the unsupportive and negative friends in your life. That's right. Unfortunately, some of the people closest to you might actually be the problem. We know you care what they think. That's okay. But did you choose them wisely? Are they supportive of your ultimate purpose in life? Or are they threatened by your success, afraid that if you reach out and pursue something better, they might have to also?

Take it from us: when you make the decision to take control of your future—to break free from the norm and challenge the status quo—all bets are off. You never know what your friends and family will do. Some will support you; others will join you. Some will reject you; others will ignore you. Some will ridicule you to your face, others behind your back. Whatever the case, it has everything to do with them, and nothing to do with you.

The real question is not whether your friends are impressed with you, but whether you are impressed with you. Did you accomplish everything you set out to? Are you achieving everything you're capable of? Are you living the life of your dreams? If you're not, then you're most likely working for someone who is.

Besides, who cares if your friends think you're a fool for trying network marketing? *We* think they're fools for not trying network marketing. And why would you take advice from someone who isn't living the life you want anyway?

Don't bother with people who criticize your effort to secure a better life for you and your family. That's not what friends do. Remember, misery loves company. And misery will do anything to get it, including disguising itself as care and concern. So don't buy into it. Don't take the bait. Your loved ones—while trying to be protective—can be some of the most disabling forces around. As we said in the introduction, we know this first-hand.

In the end, only you can decide how committed you are to living the life you want. If you're willing to get the true reward of ultimate happiness—whether through network marketing or any other endeavor—the price of admission is always the same: Your ego. For you to get in, it has to stay *out*.

> Don't unknowingly appoint your friends as designated drivers of your life. If you don't worry about your future, no one else will. Your friends will struggle far more with your financial success than they will with your hardships.
>
> Dr. Tom Barrett, Author and Network Marketing Expert

Take our word for it—it's impossible to flip your mindset around people who have the exact same mindset *you used to have*. So if you want evidence that network marketing will work for you, align yourself with the people who've made it work for them, not the ones who haven't. Or worse, the ones who haven't even tried.

And while we're at it, unless you love it, don't stick with your current job just because you're good at it. Or because it's what you do, who you are, or what you went to school for. Don't underestimate yourself. You're good at a lot of things. Those things are waiting for you.

So there you have it. If you're not willing to get over yourself, get a dream, get going, and get a great life, then we have just one last request: *Please* get out of the way for those who are.

Conclusion

We didn't write this book just to get in your face about your life, or to pick on your friends and your job. We promise. We wrote it because we care, and because we want you to know what we know so that you can have what so many of us in this profession have—a truly prosperous and joyful life.

Too many people are censoring their hopes and dreams these days, silencing that inner voice inside of them demanding to know *"Is this all there is?"* It's not. We know it's not. But don't take our word for it. Find out for yourself.

It's time to get your feet off the ground and put your head in the clouds. It's time to dust off that pipe dream and take it out for a spin. It's time to evaluate the menu of options in front of you and feel empowered to say, "No thanks. I'd like to order something different—something *better.*" You deserve it. All of it. And you deserve it now, not *someday.*

We can't promise that network marketing will make you rich, or that it will be a breeze. We can't promise that people won't ridicule your decision to do it or tell you to "Dream on." But we can promise you that if you lock arms with us—and the millions of people all around the world just like us—it will be well worth the ride.

Don't wonder what will happen if you fail. Wonder what will happen if you succeed. There's far more around the bend than you ever imagined is possible. Consider this book your fork in the road. It's up to you to take the turn.

Flip-Flop CEO Stories

Amy Cassidy, Flip Flop CEO

Masters of Science in Nursing
Nurse Practitioner
Network Marketer

My husband and I have always had a standing rule in our marriage: Anytime one of our friends approached us about one of those network marketing "opportunities," we would tell them we would always support them, but never sign up to join. Ever. I honestly looked down my nose at network marketing and thought that I was too good to ever do it. I felt like I had worked too hard and come too far in my career as a nurse practitioner to ever lower my morals and join one of "those" companies. Isn't that terrible? I actually thought those things. Well, shame on me.

I didn't become intrigued until I saw one of my good friends succeeding in her network marketing business in ways I could hardly believe. She talked to me about it, but my defenses were still up and very strong at the time. I gave her every excuse I could. But then a turning point came: After working seven, twelve-hour shifts straight, I decided maybe this whole working-to-the-point-of-exhaustion thing wasn't the only way to provide for my family. You see, I had a baby and a three-year-old at home at the time. Working those seven days straight meant I didn't even get to see my children—living under my own roof—for seven days!

I joined a network marketing business without knowing anything about my company's products, nothing about the business, and still having some pre-conceived notions regarding network marketing.

Being on the inside of network marketing for almost three years now, I have retired myself from ever working outside of the home again. Oh yeah, and my husband is now home too! We're only in our mid-30s. We are traveling the world with our two precious children, and serving our community in ways we never even thought possible. We feel blessed to be a blessing to others, and are so grateful our defenses were lowered to where we could truly see the opportunity network marketing had waiting for us.

Amy's Words of Wisdom

Consistency is key. With my company, our products are only available online, so I remind my team to talk about their website every single day. With brick and mortar stores, it's clear if the store exists or not. With a virtual business, no one knows your store is there unless talk about it every day.

So that post on social media first thing in the morning is our way of turning on the neon "open" sign on the entrance of our online store. As soon as you stop talking about your business, everyone will forget you have it, or will assume you've quit. Don't stop talking about your products or your business. Your residual income will thank you for it.

Denice Chenault, Flip-Flop CEO

BA, Communications
Personal Development Leader
Sales Rep, Network Marketer

I am the daughter of two teachers, and grew up in an idyllic setting in Colorado, with pine trees, fresh air, and lots of possibility. My younger sister and I loved horses. From the time I was ten—until I went to college—I spent every moment that I wasn't in school, on the back of a horse. I was always taught that my love for horses was a *rich man's sport!* Since we weren't rich, this meant that I had to work to support my passion. I saddled and exercised horses, braided their manes... anything I could do to earn a few bucks.

At eighteen, I went to the University of Colorado, majoring in communications and minoring in anthropology. While my dad had aspirations of me being a teacher, I envisioned myself as more of an entrepreneur... maybe a Realtor. My dad wasn't going for it, so I revoked my outrageous idea and continued my studies.

After college, I got married, and worked for a company that provided corporate training to companies. During that time, I took a personal development course that was life changing; I discovered my desire to become an instructor.

In that defining moment, I thought to myself, "This terrifies me and excites me all at the same time." I was accepted into the program and became the company's youngest instructor, and led courses all over the United States and Israel, with my now ex-husband. People say we have a better relationship, divorced, than most people who are married.

It was three years after being divorced that I met my soon to be husband, Tom. At the time, I was a sales rep for a well-known hair care company, on a 100% commission salary, and had no other income stream. As a single mom to my son, Dominic, it was a very tough time. There were weeks that I only had $20 to buy groceries. We ate lots of grilled cheese sandwiches and tomato soup. My car had been repossessed, and I was driving my grandmother's old, faded Volvo. Very sexy. I couldn't even afford cable TV, so I read lots of books.

Tom was the one who introduced me to network marketing, and I immediately loved the business model. I knew that if I learned how to build relationships, this was a way I could help other single moms just like me. Tom and I decided to really *learn* the business so we could teach it to others. Fast forward seventeen years, and we now make over a million dollars a year. But that isn't the best part. The *great* news is that we now have hundreds of thousands of people on our team who have changed their lives through this profession too. That is the true gift of what we do!

Denice's Words of Wisdom

Start by genuinely loving people and building relationships with them. Switch your mindset from *selling* to *serving*. When you serve others and do what is in *their* best interest, you remove your own agenda. Take the time to learn this profession. Treat this business seriously, so that you can learn to lead your team to success, rather than off a cliff! Network marketing gives you the opportunity to truly create a life you love!

Romi Neustadt, Flip-Flop CEO

BA, Journalism and Political Science
Trial Attorney
Network Marketer

I took a rather circuitous route to network marketing. After graduating from college and earning my law degree, I enjoyed a successful career as a trial attorney for three years. While I loved aspects of trial work, the adversarial nature of the profession began to take its toll. So I quit my job, packed my things, and moved to New York City to pursue my second career—marketing and public relations.

For twelve years, I was an agency executive in New York and Seattle. I worked hard and won awards for the communications programs I designed for Fortune 500 companies, international nonprofits, and entertainment clients.

All of that changed when my husband and I discovered we were having our first baby. I'd grown up in Montana, and wanted to give my children the gift of the small-town childhood I had. So we decided to take the plunge and move "back home." I left my job and started my own public relations consulting firm, while my husband grew his medical practice from our new locale.

For a while, it was nice to be self-employed. I was able to plan my days around my son's schedule, and still maintain my high-profile status in the public relations and marketing worlds. But when I had my second child, this time a daughter, I had an epiphany about what my next career would be.

Although our businesses were thriving—I was a nationally recognized public relations consultant, while my husband was a nationally recognized physician—we were still facing the same fate that millions of other people face— we couldn't get ahead. By the time we were done paying for the student loans, the Montessori school, the mortgage, and the bills, we couldn't fully fund our retirement accounts or the kids' college funds, let alone something extra for the life of adventure we'd always dreamed of. So I went looking for something else, although I didn't yet know what.

Around that time, a PR client of mine who was launching a fantastic jewelry line told me she'd funded her entire business from the earnings of a new network marketing company. When I found out which company she was with, I looked into it, and jumped right in.

Prior to that, I didn't have an opinion on network marketing one way or another. I was always too focused on my other careers to give it a thought. But when I saw the financial freedom it brought my client, I immediately knew it could do the same for me. That was 20 months ago. Today, I'm at the top of that company.

There are so many reasons why I love network marketing. First, my life is no longer governed by the billable hour. Instead, I make a multi-six-figure income off the hours of thousands of individual people. And I, in turn, help them do the same. But although the money and all the other perks are great, it's not the best part. The best part about network marketing is that it allows me to touch people's lives, to help them achieve their goals and become better versions of themselves. And that's what they do for me.

Romi's Words of Wisdom

I'm not at the top of my company because I'm a lawyer or former PR consultant. I'm at the top because I'm 100% coach-able and I'm hungry. It doesn't matter what skill set you have when you begin. No one is born knowing how to do this business. You just have to be willing to learn it.

Kyle and Kierston Kirschbaum, Flip-Flop CEOs

Marketing, Brigham Young University
BS, Business Management, SDSU
Kierston: Real Estate
Kyle: Internet Marketing
Network Marketers

We started our network marketing career pretty slowly, maybe much like a lot of people do. Our best friend invited us to a natural healthcare class, so out of respect for her, we went. Luckily, we learned a lot and we fell in love with the products right away! At that time, however, Kyle was running a multi-million dollar Internet marketing firm. I had a fun part-time real estate career and was pregnant with our third son.

One fateful day, our lives changed. Kyle's business suddenly went under and we were forced to borrow money from family, move out of our new home, and start over. We were faced with the grim prospects of either trying to start a new business from scratch, go find "jobs," or to actually give this network marketing thing a try. Fortunately, we chose option number three! The thought of having a boss was a huge turnoff for us. Network marketing, however, offered us a way to own our own business, work with amazing mentors, and start a business with lots of potential for growth! Our recipe for success started with a few key things.

Kyle and Kierston's Words of Wisdom

1. Create a vision board. The top of our board has the quote that we've lived by for the past couple of years: "There are two primary choices in life: to accept conditions as they exist, or to accept the responsibility for changing them." We're so grateful we chose the latter!

2. Find a mentor in the business and DO WHAT THEY SAY! Ask them for help. Learn from the great minds in the business. Let successful people in your organization know how hungry you are to work hard and to be a key player on their team. Let them know you want gasoline poured on your fire!

3. Spend thirty minutes per day working on personal development, including reading motivational books, and listening to CDs that will help you gain the skills necessary to be successful in this business.

4. Treat this like the real business that it actually is! Respect your work hours and remember that businesses make

money, but hobbies cost money. Is this your network marketing hobby?

5. Find someone on your team to mentor and teach him or her how to do what you've done, and then teach that person to mentor others!

This business is truly amazing! Even in our other successful businesses, we've never had the time and financial freedom to do what we do now. Some days we choose to travel and teach people how to improve their lives. Other days we choose to relax at home with our awesome kids. Whatever we choose, we're always wearing our "Flip-Flops!"

There is one word that sums up our lives in network marketing: FREEDOM!

Iain Pritchard, Flip Flop CEO
Property Development
Interior Design, Actor
Network Marketer

My journey with network marketing really began in February of 2008. I had little desire to sell products, I had no experience in network marketing, and I had no time. So I guess you could say this wasn't for me. However, things were changing in the world economy and my business was about to get hit like many others.

I had been part of the recent property boom, had built a residential portfolio, and had run my own successful property development and interior design business. I had been fortunate to benefit from the huge rising UK property market. I enjoyed what I did and the lifestyle it had given me along the way. Although I didn't realize it at the time, I was about to need it.

Once I understood the profession, I realized this would be the vehicle for me to leverage my time and give me opportunity to create "right now" money as well as residual income with a company that was about to globalize on a massive scale. I immediately jumped in.

Network marketing can work for everyone. It is the level playing field that can give the ordinary person an extraordinary life by simply redirecting their spending and teaching others to do the same. I love how this concept works. It's exactly the same as any corporate structure except that in network marketing, everyone has the same opportunity to benefit from the leverage. Instead of the money going into different corporations' pockets, it is being shared among the individuals building networks.

This is the business model of the 21st century. It rewards effort. More and more companies are using this model as a low overhead and legitimate vehicle to distribute products and services. With online ordering at an all-time high and technology changing the way we all do business and live our lives, this is the future, and network marketing is my vehicle.

This is an opportunity to be paid a generous income as a result of an initial introduction to the products and concept. It's being paid for your word-of-mouth advertising that has the potential to pay you again and again for your initial referral. Network marketing is different things to different people. For some, it's a Plan B; for others, its ends up becoming their Plan A. It can also be a brilliant exit strategy from the corporate world or give people a chance to be more present in their children's lives.

My dreams weren't for sale and no one was going to tell me otherwise. I had to decide whether I was going to listen to successful people who had proven this business could work or the narrow-minded friend or family member who was quick to tell me I was mad, even though they didn't have the lifestyle I wanted. I had a gift to share with others—to help change lives by sharing how to build a network marketing business, develop leaders, and empower individuals.

Please ask yourself this: What in the world would stop me from doing this? Do I have everything I want? Is my mortgage paid off? Do I have enough invested to pay me for life when I retire? If my principle income stream stopped tomorrow, how long could I survive on my savings?

Iain's Words of Wisdom

Don't be the one who missed the boat because you allowed fears, excuses, lack of time, knowledge, or self-belief to get in your way. We all have twenty-four hours in a day. We just need to use them wisely. Treat this as a business and get paid like one. Treat it as a "little thing on the side," and that's what you will get paid. Your business will be as BIG as your vision. I am proof. Proof that in hard economic times, being time poor, having little knowledge of this profession and no degree, I could build a six-figure income part-time, alongside everything else I do.

Britney Beneke, Flip-Flop CEO
BS, Marketing & Communications
Recreation Community Education Manager
Network Marketer

Growing up, we moved a lot, which is how I learned the gift of gab. I was constantly being tossed into a roomful of strangers, forcing me to learn how to make friends easily. That experience has made me value and hold onto relationships, even when we're miles apart. I love connecting with people, and genuinely get excited helping others realize that they deserve to live a life they love! It's so fun getting to know people who also crave freedom, and share my curiosity about discovering all that life has to offer. As a busy mom of two, being able to do this for a living is a dream come true, and has truly been the icing on the cake.

Ironically, this life changing journey began when I stumbled upon a post a friend made on Facebook about an amazing product that was helping her. I was feeling stuck in my life, and was really intrigued by her comments. I was already in network marketing, and was struggling, so I definitely had no intention of getting involved with another company. But once I personally experienced the amazing changes the products made, I knew I'd found something I had to share with everyone I knew.

From there, everything just snowballed. I quickly became a top leader in my company by simply sharing my own experience. Most people think you need to be good at sales to do this business, but I have never once felt like a salesperson. It's completely natural for me to share things I love with others. I do it when I discover a great restaurant, see an incredible movie, or read a good book. I'm still filled with excitement anytime I get to share this business with someone. I love talking about the time freedom that this business has given me, and I can't help but get emotional when I share the changes that are happening for our family. I've never looked at my business as being about *me* at all. I'm just an excited girl who still loves garage sales, using coupons, and sharing my great finds with others. I feel like if I don't share this amazing opportunity, someone who really needs it might not ever know that it exists.

This industry is full of remarkable opportunities with world-class products. As the corporate world continues to change—with downsizing and outsourcing—I'm confident that this business is the answer for so many families. One of the things that I love most about this business is that you can do it from anywhere. We live "in the sticks" of Iowa, where we need a satellite dish just to access the internet. So, if I can do this, anyone can!

Britney's Words of Wisdom

Don't stop searching until you find whatever it is that gives you that feeling of butterflies. Of excitement so strong that you wake up each morning feeling like you can't wait to jump out of bed and share it. *That* is what will ignite your passion. There's nothing in this world that can take that from you. Allow your confidence to be fueled by those that you are helping along the way. When your "me" turns to "we," there's no stopping the amount of blessings that will surround you and your entire team.

Laura Evans, Flip-Flop CEO

College dropout
Sales & Marketing Executive
Network Marketer

My career as a sales and marketing executive spanned over 25 years, working for companies like JCrew, Disney, and even a few well-known network marketing companies. I reported directly to company owners, and was a key decision maker responsible for sales of a billion dollars in revenue for several Fortune 500 companies. I was also on the board of the Direct Selling Association and the Direct Selling Education Foundation. I was financially and professionally successful. I appeared to be the least likely person to be interested in building a network marketing business.

Yet, at the prime of my career, I walked away from it all. The money. The power. The responsibility. The glory of success. Why did I walk away?

While I appeared to have it all, on the inside, I was emotionally bankrupt. The burden of reorganizing, downsizing, and rightsizing had left me overcome with guilt, longing to be with my family and friends, after years of neglected relationships.

Working on the corporate side of major network

marketing companies had taught me, firsthand, that the network marketing business model is a legitimate and valuable form of marketing. I had even been asked to speak at universities to educate folks about how and why this industry works so well for businesses, customers, and entrepreneurs. I had celebrated the success stories of ordinary people (like me) who'd accomplished extraordinary results and achieved financial independence through their network marketing businesses. Unlike many people, no one had to persuade me about the legitimacy of network marketing. I just needed to find the courage, and thoughtfully create my exit strategy from the Corporate America treadmill.

Finally, in January of 2014, I walked away from a lifestyle that was all about designing my life around my work, and into network marketing, where life and work can peacefully coexist, free of the constant conflict of having to choose one over the other.

Why did I make this choice? Because I finally woke up to the fact that in my twenty years of being a mom to four amazing children, I'd missed each of my children's first days of school, their field trips, special events, parades, and recitals. Within my first week of my new-found freedom, I attended my first field trip. The face of my ten-year-old son Jack, beaming as I drove him and his friends to a musical play, was priceless!

I was able to organize an 80th birthday party for my mom, and finally celebrate her birthday the way she had celebrated so many of mine. I was able to spend more time with her in the last two years of her life on Earth than I had in the twenty years prior. Again, priceless!

The privilege of being present in the new and existing relationships in my life has been…priceless! I now have the pleasure of introducing products and the business I love with others. I get to share the concepts of feeling better, improving the quality of one's life, experiencing more fun with less worry, and designing a life you love.

I am not saying everyone needs to walk away from their job. But for me it was the right decision. I decided that rather than building someone else's business, it was time for me to build my own. I now lead a passionate team representing over $3 million in annual sales, and am traveling the world on expense-paid vacations with my family. I'm finally living a life I absolutely love.

Laura's Words of Wisdom

1. Make a decision. Decide what you want to create. Don't worry about the how—it will reveal itself once

you make the decision. Making a decision empowers your subconscious to help you attract the results.

2. Focus on details about the future you want. Visualize what it will feel like, who'll be with you, what you'll wear, and what you'll say. The more detailed your vision, the more easily you'll attract results.

3. Relationships matter. In the words of Theodore Roosevelt: "People don't care how much you know until they know how much you care." We have a gift to share, so become a better listener. Care more about what the other person needs, rather than what you need from them. The rest will fall into place.

Loren Robin, Flip-Flop CEO

Top 1% Realtor Nationwide, Licensed Broker,
Certified International Property and Luxury
Home Marketing Specialist
Network Marketer

While working a dream job for a real estate developer, I sold some big, amazing homes to people who'd been very successful in network marketing—something I hadn't heard of before, so I was curious. They shared two reasons they loved network marketing: residual income and time freedom.

I had neither one in my real estate business, so those reasons got my attention.

While I sensed that someday I might have an interest, at that point I was not interested. As a single mother, I felt blessed to be earning so much money and providing a good life for my twin sons. Compared to the benefits, the sacrifices seemed unimportant. I worked seven days a week leaving little time for family and my health. Unfortunately, my best year financially was my worst year personally. I did not own my own life.

I kept rolling along, until the south Florida real estate crash in 2006. Suddenly, my income was plummeting. With my sons in college and my debts mounting, I had nothing to draw upon except my own personal resources.

Remembering the network marketing success stories of those early real estate clients, I decided to follow my heart, reinvent myself, and join the network marketing industry.

As a top Realtor, I knew the importance of getting into massive action: burning up the phones, meetings every day, and talking to people constantly.

But this time, my actions were powered by a deep belief in our industry where, implausible as it may sound, you earn a living by being the best you can be and showing others how to do the same thing. It's amazing to watch the rewards that follow.

Today, my organization includes more than 17,000 distributors, which generates more than $1 million in monthly volume. But the reward I value most is freedom.

In 2012, I felt free to leave Florida and to move to San Diego so I could be close to my sons. I used to receive a large commission check when I sold a property. Today, I receive an even larger check every month as residuals from my network marketing business. I feel so blessed by the freedom it gives me—freedom to be close to my sons and the freedom to live in a beautiful spot overlooking the beach, with amazing views of the sunsets from my home office. It's a dream come true.

That's what time freedom and residual income really mean—having the time, resources, and freedom to make your dreams come true. My intent is to show others how to receive this freedom... so more of us can live the kind of life we deserve.

Loren's Words of Wisdom

Listen closely to the thousands of life-changing success stories told throughout the network marketing industry. They are real. Ask yourself, "Is what I am doing today ever going to get me the time freedom and residual income I deserve?"

When you align your career with your true purpose, you'll never work another day in your life!

Amanda Graves, Flip-Flop CEO

BS, Business Administration
Banker
Network Marketer

My journey into network marketing initially began as a way to escape an abusive marriage. The meetings and opportunity events gave me a chance to connect with positive, upbeat women who were successful. Although my business wasn't successful, I took advantage of the training as a way to grow myself.

After divorcing and becoming a single mom, I decided to join another network marketing company as a way to pay for childcare, so I could work a full-time job. I was a bit more successful with my second company. I worked my business, attended trainings, conferences, and continued to learn as much as I could.

After remarrying, my second husband was offered a great job in his home state. Because of the ability to do my business from anywhere, I was able to easily pick up my new budding business, and move it with us. I soon became pregnant and found myself less enthusiastic about the company I was with, so I began to pray for guidance about where to look next.

I remember sitting at my kitchen table during my

3rd trimester, and checking out the DSA (Direct Sales Association) website. All I wanted was to be able to give our girls a backyard play set and have a little extra "fun money" for manicures and shopping. While browsing the list of companies, I saw one that sounded interesting, and instantly felt a weight lifted. I knew this was what I had been searching for, and it was less than a $100 investment! I immediately joined the company, and have been on an amazing ride ever since!

Being in network marketing has helped me regain a sense of who I am, which tends to get lost sometimes in the process of taking care of everyone else. I am still a mommy and a wife, but I am also a successful business woman. Throughout my next pregnancy, I consistently worked my business, doing a little each day. I have found that if I just continue taking small, consistent steps, over time the payoff in this business is huge!

During the first four and a half years of our marriage, my husband worked about three hours away, and was only home two nights a week. I continued to work my business, and eventually, my commissions and overrides were enough to pay our bills and allow us to enjoy an amazing new lifestyle. Thanks to my business, my husband was able to become a stay-at-home dad, and has the flexibility to work when he wants to.

Even though my first two network marketing companies didn't pan out, I gleaned as much knowledge as I could and it eventually paid off. We have been truly blessed through network marketing, being able to travel together with our children and extended family, meeting amazing people all over the world, and being able to give to charities and mission work that are close to our heart.

It is amazing that a less than $100 investment has allowed me to live a life that I once only dreamed of. Now I feel called upon to use these blessings to empower other women around the world to believe that they, too, can achieve their dreams and live a life they love.

Amanda's Words of Wisdom

Don't make excuses; don't put off what can be done today, and never pre-judge!

There are five principles that have been key to my success:

1. Set goals—no matter how small.
2. Build relationships.
3. Have a positive outlook and attitude. "Attitude determines Altitude."

4. Work even when you don't feel like it.
5. Work now, play later—Work like a captain, play like a pirate!

Margie and Ashley Aliprandi, Flip-Flop CEOs

Margie: BA, Music Education,
Junior High Music Teacher
Ashley: BA, Fine Arts, Model, Singer, Dancer
Network Marketers

Margie's Story

I started my network marketing business in 1989 with seemingly three strikes against me: I had no business experience, no capital to get started, and I was a single mom with three little kids. But I wanted to give my kids a better life. They became my reason for saying "yes" when an exciting product came my way. It was a product I knew I could talk about with anyone, anytime, anywhere. I was passionate about it. So I opted not to go back to teaching. I began a network marketing journey that changed many lives... including mine. The best thing I did was to make a "whatever it takes" decision. In the beginning, I couldn't afford to fly so I drove all over the US to do meetings with my team. I slept in my car and used gas station bathrooms to get ready.

After the initial sacrifices, challenges, and a year of

focused work, I was making more in a month than I could make in a year of teaching. Within three years—at age thirty-five—I had earned my first million dollars. Twenty-seven years later, in 2016, I have a team of more than 250,000 spanning twenty-nine countries. I've been listed among the top one percent of network marketing earners worldwide, traveled extensively with my four children, and experienced the deeper personal development that our magnificent business model requires.

Because of network marketing, I've been able to work from home, offer my children the right opportunities, and help them excel. I've enjoyed the time freedom. I've helped others break through their fears and step into greater strength, confidence, and financial security. Where else besides network marketing does all this come together so beautifully? I started this business to give my four children an extraordinary life. Mission accomplished! It gives me tremendous joy when I think about the ripple effect that my "whatever it takes" decision has had on the lives of people all over the world. Just recently, my youngest daughter, Ashley, decided to join me in my network marketing business. I am having the time of my life building this business with my precious daughter at my side.

Ashley's Story

My mother has created one of the largest network marketing teams in the world. I watched her as a single mother not only make sacrifices for her dreams, but also experience the satisfaction of what our profession has to offer. I was a recipient of the lifestyle, so by the time I came along, things were easy; I never had to experience the struggle. I was able to travel around the world, get a great education, and because my mother was pursuing her dreams, I learned that mine really mattered. I remember her saying, "I will pay you not to get a job." She didn't pay me, but that idea was planted, and it kept my wheels turning. I was determined to find a way to be an entrepreneur and to create a significant life of contribution.

So I went to college, double majored, and wrote a book, all in an attempt to make my life grand and do what I thought I was supposed to do. But something continued to eat away at me. I had three objectives for my life. Number one, I wanted to be my own boss. Number 2, I wanted to make an unlimited amount of money. Number 3, I wanted to help a lot of people and make a difference in this world. Looking at the jobs my friends were getting, it didn't seem possible. While I was jealous of the immediate money they were making, that path felt so limited—so slave-to-the-man—to me. How would I ever be able to achieve my three objectives?

Well, the stars must have been aligned because it was nearing the time of graduation and my mother invited me to attend an event. I had attended thousands of events all over the world to support my mother, but this time, her company of 27 years was rebranding and this was the official relaunch. The look, feel, and sound of the brand were entirely different. I could relate to the people who walked on the stage; I was inspired by their vision and integrity. I remember grabbing my mother's hand and whispering in her ear, "What has been in front of me my entire life is actually my destiny."

I've jumped in with both feet, and know that with consistent work, one day I will achieve success just as my mother has. All of my life experiences up until now have been preparation for this. I'm fulfilling the three objectives I've had for my life. I'm my own boss. I have the ability to make an unlimited amount of money, and I am certain that every day we are helping a lot of people and making a positive difference in the world.

Margie's Words of Wisdom

Stay! I did. Even when people all around me were saying, "No."

Persist! There's a sowing season and a reaping season,

and they don't occur at the same time. Your job is to keep planting. If you plant consistently, every day, the harvest will come. And when it comes, you'll have two contrasting feelings at once: A quiet knowing that you've paid the price, and overwhelming gratitude that jumps up and asks, "What did I do to deserve this?"

Ashley's Words of Wisdom

When your purpose shifts from personal ambition to altruistic conviction, only then are you unstoppable. Lead with your heart and trust the process; your success is assured.

Amber Voight, Flip-Flop CEO
High School Dropout
Network Marketer

I have to begin by saying that if I can be successful in this business, anyone can be! My wonderful husband and I were married at just seventeen and had our first son when we were eighteen. Instead of thinking about prom or graduation like the other kids our age, we were busy planning our family. We both dropped out of high school so that we could go to work.

I worked in retail every night and every weekend and never got to see my son or my husband. I was desperately looking for a way out of my situation when I discovered direct sales/network marketing at a craft expo. When I heard that you could be your own boss and set your own hours, I was so excited that I immediately jumped in!

Unfortunately, I learned pretty quickly that it wasn't quite as simple as just signing up. I wasn't offered a lot of support or guidance, and I ended up failing miserably! I refused to give up, though. I just kept thinking about my son and the lifestyle I wanted for him and continued to do everything I could to succeed. I jumped from one company to another, thinking I would finally find success at the newest, "latest and greatest" company—but it still didn't happen! Everyone I knew told me to give up and get a real job. But somehow I believed that I could do this. I kept seeing other people achieve success—so I just kept thinking, *Why not me?*

After lots and lots of disappointment and failure, I finally decided that maybe it was me that was the problem... maybe I needed to change something about myself to be successful. One of the things that so many of the leaders in the business would talk about was the importance of working on ourselves first. I'd never even heard the words "personal development" before that. I can't believe it took me so long to realize that I just might be the problem.

By this time, our lives were pretty much a mess. We had 3 little boys, our cars had just been repossessed, we were on food support, and we were about to lose our home. Finally, I began to understand that I was failing because I wasn't ready to succeed yet. So, I immediately got to work, determined to turn our lives around! I began reading anything and everything I could get my hands on about leadership, dealing with people, and the profession of network marketing. I quickly started to notice not only a change in myself but a change in my business, as well.

Suddenly money started coming in, people were joining

my team—it was working! A year later, I was able to go from hopeless, on welfare, and almost homeless to moving into our dream home. My husband was able to retire at 28, and I have grown a team of 23,000 women who are selling more than $2 million dollars a month in product. And, I've even been featured in *Networking Times*, our industry's premier publication. We now are financially free and live life on our terms—because I never gave up.

Amber's Words of Wisdom

"You have to grow yourself before your checks will grow."

Amber Voight

Never, ever give up on your dreams... ever! You can do this. You can do anything that you decide to do!

Gary M. Lindner, Flip-Flop CEO

BS, Arizona State University
MS, Washington State University
PhD in Physiology, Clemson University
University of California Davis, Faculty
California State University - Chico, Adjunct Professor
Co-Founder Bio-Tech Company: Applied Genetics
Network Marketer

Go to school, get an education, find something you're passionate about, be the best at it, and you will make lots of money. This was the advice of my parents. I followed this advice to the letter.

I was that person on every network marketer's chicken list. Educated, successful in business, and seemingly happy. No one ever approached me about a network marketing opportunity.

I came across network marketing by happenstance. During an extended business trip, an individual told me about a Japanese company with products that might help a severe neck issue I had been dealing with for three years. I politely (or maybe it wasn't so politely) told him that I had no interest in alternative products for health.

End of story!

Two days later, I was reading our local paper and came across an article about the same company that this young man had mentioned. Maybe, just maybe, I didn't know everything? Maybe the universe was trying to tell me something? Ya think?

I decided to do a little research and was astonished when a literature search revealed corroboration for the products' efficacy. Since the only medical option for my injury was neck surgery, I located a distributor for the company in a nearby town and bought a few products. Astonishingly, they worked. I was then informed, oh by the way, there was also a business opportunity.

My epiphany came during a long business trip, while my wife was giving me a play-by-play account of my son's Little League game. Why was it that I had worked so hard to create a successful company, but couldn't be there for my son's game? It appeared that my beloved company didn't love me back.

This elicited some real soul-searching and evaluation as to what I really wanted. I wanted to be at school plays, birthdays, holidays, and family dinners!

Here I am, 16 years later, a professional network marketer being reminded daily that I made the right choice for myself and my family. It has allowed me the time freedom to become the father I wanted to be. I love network marketing and am passionate to share this gift with others. This is an incredible industry that can rekindle dreams and awaken the spirit to be more. I appreciate my role as a leader to inspire and empower others to fulfill their own dreams.

Dr. Gary's Words of Wisdom

Do your own due diligence. If you want success, this business is about building a network of distribution, not simply selling a product.

If there is a moral to my story, it is not to prejudge your prospects. You never know who is looking, no matter what the outward appearance. Share your message with conviction and passion and be the leader to inspire others to be all they can be.

Ask questions, listen, and provide solutions!

Pam Barnum, Flip-Flop CEO

BA (Hons.), MPA, JD
Federal Crown Prosecutor
Network Marketer

Before being introduced to network marketing, I enjoyed some pretty amazing career experiences. I actually met my husband working as an undercover police officer (just so you don't think I married a drug dealer, my husband Kevin was also an undercover officer at the time).

I realized that buying drugs and working away from home wasn't a very "family friendly" job, so I went to law school, became a lawyer, and worked as a federal prosecuting attorney. Turns out that working sixty to seventy hours a week is not all that "family friendly" either.

Kevin and I were living the dream, working in a secure job with benefits and a pension plan, earning more than a quarter of a million dollars in salaries—and we never saw each other.

One day, a neighbor told me about a product she was using. I agreed to buy it and offhandedly, she said, "By the way, it's network marketing!" I had no idea what network marketing was, but Kevin seemed to because he whispered under his breath, "We don't want anything to do with that.

Our garage will be full and we'll have no friends left." Still clueless, I ordered the products.

So how did I go from earning a six-figure income as a lawyer to earning a multiple six-figure income as a network marketer in eighteen months? Well, I have my son to thank for that.

One day, as I was hurrying to get my then five-year-old son ready for school, he looked up at me and asked, "Mommy, are we in a hurry again today?" It was like a knife went through my heart. I realized that what I was communicating to my son was that my job was my priority— not my family— and nothing could have been further from the truth. I had never understood the philosophy behind your "why" until that moment. Spending time with my son was and still is my "why."

I realized that day that the *dream* is really about family and the freedom you get when you control your own destiny instead of waiting for someone else to do that for you. I am privileged to be a part of the evolved economy better known as network marketing.

Pam's Words of Wisdom

My network marketing journey has taught me that there

are really three main "secrets" to network marketing success:

1. Connect with your "why." Your "why" should be so vivid and compelling that it excites you to work your business every day.
2. Be a product of your products and communicate your passion to at least three new people each day.
3. Be driven by integrity, not money. You can always earn more money, but your integrity is priceless.

Vanessa and Adam Green, Flip-Flop CEO

Vanessa: College dropout
Waitress
Adam: Kinesiology Diploma
Personal Trainer
Network Marketers

I was first introduced to network marketing in 2012 when I was eighteen and a waitress. I'd reluctantly attended an opportunity event with my mother who had to *drag* me there. Little did I know that I was about to meet my future husband, Adam Green, at that meeting. While I was interested in the company's opportunity, I was mostly interested in the gentleman I'd just met. I pursued my new crush, and we started dating a few months later. Seeing the amazing success that Adam, my sister, and my mom were creating with the business, I decided I'd start sharing the products as well. I did this while continuing to waitress part time. I set a goal to replace my monthly waitressing income, and one year later I was able to reach that goal.

Meanwhile, Adam's business was growing very quickly. Within two short years, his business had grown from 600 to 18,000 members. Adam grew his business by focusing on the "young mom market," and leveraged his time by using the power of duplication.

In June 2014, we "tied the knot." During that same month, we experienced the real benefit of residual income, earning our highest paycheck ever while taking the entire month off. Because we'd worked very hard for the first few years, we were able to focus on and enjoy some of the important things in life—like getting married and honeymooning. We now build our businesses together. Adam is the driving force of the business, and I support him in the relational role with our team. Because of this business, I've also been given the time and financial freedom to pursue my dream of investing a year in Bible School.

Together, we have had opportunities to travel to over ten countries as a newly married couple. We build our business wherever we go, and are enjoying the adventure along the way. We have also been able to support some of our favorite organizations in building houses for the extremely poor, and financing a rescue center for babies who have been rescued from the dump. Because of the gift of network marketing, God has given us the opportunity to give away what we used to make annually in our regular jobs. Today, our business is comprised of thirty-five thousand team members globally, and we're earning a seven-figure annual income.

Vanessa and Adam's Words of Wisdom

Commit a minimum of four years to your business. You would expect to commit four years to earning a degree in order to earn a professional-level income. You need to treat this business in exactly the same manner.

Cecilia Stoll, Flip-Flop CEO
BS, Psychology
Secretary
Network Marketer

One of my favorite songs says that faith is stepping out onto nothing and landing on something. In July 1991, I was working as a secretary. Even with my psychology degree, that was the only job I could get at the time. I was frustrated with the eight-to-five routine and the "paycheck-to-paycheck" mentality to which my husband and I had grown accustomed. We had no money for vacations or extra things. When I envisioned my life five years down the road, things looked bleak. I knew that when we started our family, I wanted to be able to stay home with our kids. We knew that becoming a one-income family would be a serious lifestyle change for us. However, if I kept doing what I was doing, I would continue to get what I was getting. I had to do something, but I did not know what until God brought an angel into my life.

A dear friend introduced me to network marketing. At first, I dabbled just to get my products at a discount and I sold products to a few friends. After about six months, I realized I had the potential to not only make some extra money but to replace my full-time income.

It wasn't always a smooth ride, but it was worth all the sacrifices. I struggled with everything everyone else struggles with while building my business: rejection, cancellations, no-shows, people's lack of belief in me and this opportunity, time away from home, late nights and early mornings. For a long time, I was the only person on my team who was committed enough to go to meetings. I was a team of one, but I did not give myself the option to quit. I think it is normal to ask, "Will this ever work for me?" "Are all of the sacrifices I am making going to pay off someday?" or "Why doesn't anyone want this as badly as I do?"

I have learned so much along the way. I learned that it is better to get serious than it is to just "play" with your business every now and then. I learned that if you are not "coachable," you will not be a great coach. I learned that even though in the beginning you spend money to build your business, there comes a day when, with one pay check from network marketing, you can have the potential to pay off all your bills and have plenty left over. I learned that unless you are willing to grow personally, your potential for income will not grow.

What has network marketing allowed our family to experience? I can't even begin to describe what financial freedom has brought into our lives. I love that my husband was able to let his mom choose her retirement home after my father-in-law passed away; I love that my kids attend a private Christian school; I love that I can help my mom, who lives in Brazil, with her medical expenses and with flights to and from the United States; I love that my family and I get to go to Africa on mission trips together; I love that we have the opportunity to give back and make a difference in the lives of other people.

This business has given me incredible gifts in addition to financial freedom. The two that stand out in my mind are personal growth and friendships. My journey of personal growth has been amazing. I am hardly the person I was when I joined this business. If it all ended today, I know that because of my experiences with network marketing, I am a better wife, mom, and friend because of what I have learned through this business. I would not trade it for anything because I am now living my dream life.

Cecilia's Words of Wisdom

My words for someone who is considering this business are simple: Jump in with both feet! I love that the most successful people in this business considered themselves "ordinary," yet accomplished extraordinary things. This business will not only change your life, but it will give you the opportunity to bless the lives of those who God puts in your path. You will become a better person just for being on this journey. It is *more* than worth it!

Jules Price, Flip-Flop CEO

BA, Psychology and Music
Professional Singer/Actress
Network Marketer

After living in NYC for twelve years as a professional singer and actress, my husband and I made the big decision to relocate to Sarasota, Florida where we knew no one. We were ready for a lifestyle change and wanted to live in a place with beautiful weather and turquoise water!

With no support system around, I looked online at various women's clubs, and I came in contact with a woman who invited me to join her group, but since it was an hour away, I politely declined. At the end of the brief conversation she asked, "By the way, when is your birthday? I like to send birthday cards." I shared the date with her and didn't think anything else of it. Seven months later on my birthday, I received two cards in the mail. One was from my mom, and the other was from her… and it had a $5 Starbucks gift card inside!

I called to thank her and ask why she did this, and she told me that she had a tool that allowed her to be really good at staying in touch with others to let them know she cared. I was so impressed with what she showed me, that when I learned this was something I could also share—while creating an income—I jumped in with both feet. I thought, there isn't a single person in the world who couldn't at least benefit from knowing this tool exists, and I can get paid to tell people about it? No brainer!

I'd always liked the idea of creating a residual income, but never pictured myself representing other products I'd seen. I never wanted to feel sales-y. Although I had no background in the profession, I moved forward with focus, enthusiasm, and a desire to help and support others.

Now I get to actively look for ways to celebrate and uplift people every day, and help others do so as well. It has allowed me to grow in so many aspects: As an entrepreneur, coach, mentor, speaker and writer, with the ability to affect others positively on a deeper level than I'd ever experienced as a performer. It's like a magical show that never ends.

Jules' Words of Wisdom

The main key to success is the ability to commit to doing a few simple things consistently: Share your product, give people all of their options, and help them get started as a customer or distributor… repeat! Let your passion shine through, and always maintain a strong vision for where you're going despite the obstacles that will inevitably arise.

Puya Ghandian, Flip-Flo-CEO

College Dropout
VP Business Development
Network Marketer

At 17, I discovered the world of personal development while working at a local grocery store. Instead of a cash tip, the woman I assisted gave me a personal development book. I instantly recognized the value of self improvement, and I love applying the principles from books like *Think and Grow Rich* by Napoleon Hill. In his book, Napoleon Hill says, "I learned that going the extra mile makes a difference." I implemented that truth while I was working as a receptionist at one of the fastest growing advertising firms in America. I arrived earlier and stayed later than everyone else. I was never afraid of hard work, and management took notice. Within two years—when I was 23—I became a vice president at the company, managing almost fifty people. At first I was thrilled with the promotion, but before long my life was all work and no play. I had become a slave to my job with no time for the things I enjoyed most—friends and traveling.

Then one Sunday afternoon, a friend posted a comment on Facebook about a new business venture, and I replied instantly. I had learned the importance of hanging out with people who have their stuff together, and this guy did. That's how I decided to join network marketing.

Within months, I left my previous company and jumped into my business full time. One of the things I appreciate the most is being able to set my own hours.

Today, I enjoy sharing personal-development lessons with others, and network marketing has given me the opportunity to speak to large audiences—sometimes over 40,000 people— about the importance of knowing, visualizing, and achieving one's dreams.

One of my biggest drivers is to care and provide for my family and to live life in complete abundance. That's exactly what this business has given me the opportunity to do...by simply following a system. From the beginning, I focused on adding as much value as I could to the lives of those I partner with. I've had the opportunity to contribute to over 260 people who now earn a six-figure income. Twelve of them are considered million dollar earners—and all of this has happened in less than four years.

As the great Zig Ziglar said, "You can get everything in life you want if you will just help enough other people get what they want." I've learned that dreams should be as much about fun as they are about business and financial success. I'm not all about work; like a lot of people who are in their 20s, I have a lot of fun. But thanks to the profession of network marketing, I am able to enjoy life with a lot more income than most people my age.

Puya's Words of Wisdom

Living Free, Living Happy and Living in Abundance is what life's all about! Find somebody to model and you to will begin living intentionally!

Geralyn Camarillo and Arna Johnson, Flip-Flop CEO

Gerayln: AA, Multimedia
Professional Photographer
Arna: BA, Commercial Photography
Professional Photography
Network Marketers

We're entrepreneurs at heart and have never had the desire to work a regular nine-to-five J.O.B. (which, to us, stands for **J**ust **O**ver **B**roke). As creative individuals, we each owned and operated successful award-winning professional photography businesses in Hawai'i. Both of us were earning a six-figure income.

In 2008, the unthinkable happened and we became another statistic of the economic crash. Our businesses suffered tremendously, causing both of us to file for bankruptcy and to lose our home to foreclosure. We were broke, and if it weren't for our family's rental unit being available, we would have been homeless.

The stress from the tumultuous changes took a monumental toll on us mentally, emotionally, and physically. Then, in August of 2013, we were introduced to our current company as a way to become physically healthier. We didn't know that it would also help us become financially healthier as well.

As entrepreneurs, we've always loved the freedom of creating our own schedule. The challenge as photographers, though, was that we were still trapped in the old system of trading our time for dollars. We also had the other stressful aspects of owning a small business such as overhead, employees, and marketing costs. So, although we were very successful, we recognized that if we didn't work, we wouldn't get paid. And there was no way to duplicate ourselves because we were hired for our unique artistic talents.

Throughout the years, we've kept our eye on the business model of network marketing because of the incredible benefits—mainly residual income. For the past twenty years, we've dabbled in seven different companies, but never found much success until we were blessed to partner up with our current company.

In September of 2013, we decided to pursue this new endeavor full time. Thanks to the support of our leadership team, a duplicable business system, and partnerships with passionate team members, we were able to create a six-figure income in less than a year!

There are two key components to our continued success:

#1 is having a willingness to say yes to opportunities that stretch our comfort zones, because when we grow, our business grows. We are firm believers in personal development and breaking through limiting beliefs that hold us back so that we can maximize our true potential; #2 is always operating from the heart space of helping others realize their own magnificence.

As leaders and students of the network marketing industry, we continue to enjoy the journey we're on, creating lifelong friendships, and experiencing the rewards of monthly residual income. In reflection, the greatest gifts are who we are becoming in the process, and being able to help others achieve success.

Geralyn's Words of Wisdom

Grow yourself and your business will grow. Give yourself permission to *shine*! Go out there and be your radiant self!

Arna's Words of Wisdom

You've got to believe in your company, your products, in network marketing, and most importantly yourself.

Sara Marble, Flip-Flop CEO

BS, Nursing
Registered Nurse
Network Marketer

When I started using some amazing all-natural products to help me lose a little weight after having a baby, I had no idea I had just been introduced to my future career in network marketing. I signed up with the company to get wholesale prices and at the time was totally clueless about the wonderful opportunity that had just been placed in front of me.

As a labor and delivery nurse, I was happy helping mothers bring their new babies into the world, but at the same time was disheartened with the stress it brought to our family. With me working twelve-hour night shifts, mostly on weekends, I was missing soccer games and family time while I rotated between working and sleeping.

In the hospital setting, there are no vacation days. Nights, weekends, and holidays, all have to be covered, and I would get a knot in the pit of my stomach when having to choose which of those I would spend away from my growing family.

After seeing remarkable success with these health supplements, I began sharing with my friends and family what my new favorite products were doing for me. It quickly became evident to me that I was getting compensated for recommending something that I loved! What an amazing concept! It didn't take long for me to realize that I had accidentally stumbled upon a virtual goldmine of rewards and bonuses for doing something on my own time and schedule. Within a few months, I'd generated enough income, part time, to "retire" from my registered nurse position at the hospital and focus on learning and growing in this industry of network marketing.

While pregnant with our third son, I worked from home and watched my team explode. I quickly realized that I had found a way to live my dream of staying home and raising my babies, feeling fulfilled and successful, while working at a part-time business! I had never experienced such an amazing opportunity to be part of a team that worked together to achieve goals and help others. Through this business, I am helping transform lives, both physically and financially.

If someone had told me two years ago that I would be one of the top leaders in my company in such a short time, working during my children's naps and between play dates and baseball practices, I probably would have laughed at them. Through network marketing, I am living the life I had dreamed about with my husband and our three boys. I feel overjoyed to be able to share this opportunity with others.

Sara's Words of Wisdom

Set goals and dream big. Always be willing to learn and grow. Seek out mentors and be coachable so that you can truly become the best "you" possible. The opportunities are endless if you want to work hard and help others.

Loren Slocum Lahav, Flip-Flop CEO

BA, Journalism
Author, Speaker, Personal Development
Facilitator and Coach
Network Marketer

I have always been an entrepreneur at heart. When I was nine years old, my brother and I started our first business—The Cow's Hide. We made leather belts, bracelets, and keychains, which we sold at the flea market. We worked every Saturday and Sunday, starting at 6:00 A.M. Rain or shine, we were there.

We loved it! I worked all through high school selling for Brooks Clothing, and hotdogs at the ballpark. I learned so much about listening to what people truly desired.

That has always been my passion. I pride myself on being a "connector."

I had known about network marketing since 1989, but I also had the "I'm too cool syndrome" going on. I said no for seventeen years.

The challenge was I was closed-minded and didn't take the time to understand the power of network marketing and how it was the vehicle for me to help my friends truly find their passion.

Then, in October 2007, my friend happened to be at an event where I was teaching. He overheard a conversation I was having that made him realize I needed to understand what this business had to offer, so he pulled me aside and told me we needed to chat. Once we were outside he said, "That's it...you are coming with me to our conference. Then you can give me an *educated* decision after you attend."

With three small children, I had lots of legitimate reasons not to go, but I knew if I made my kids the "excuse" versus the "reason," I would never know.

Saying YES to that conference was one of best decisions of my life.

At that conference I made a *decision*. I resolved to go "all in" and give it my very best. I grew my business while working full time, writing my second book, raising three children, and traveling 165 days a year. I disciplined myself to grow my business in stolen moments.

Our team grew to the top position faster than any other team previously had in the history of the company. I felt like Roger Banister! I was so happy because I knew that it would give people hope that it could be done!

Loren's Words of Wisdom

As my mentor says: Give it a strong yes, or a strong no, but no wishy-washy, dilly-dally stuff!

- Develop a strong belief in who you are.
- Get your fears out of the way.
- Commit to a vision. I'm obsessive about vision boards. It's the first thing I did when I committed, and I designed my board about who I needed to become to achieve success.
- Listen to successful people and be coachable.
- Create a strong "Non-Negotiable Daily Method of Operation."
- Stay hungry.
- *Always* lead by example.
- Put other people's needs above your own.
- You have heard it before: "When you help others get what they want, you will get what you want."
- Stay true to who you are.

Suzanne Van Parys, Flip-Flop CEO
BA, Psychology
Corporate Sales
Network Marketer

I grew up in a small town with loving, entrepreneurial parents who believed in me and told me that with hard work, I could do and have everything I wanted in life. So, I believed them and decided I wanted it all.

Prior to network marketing, I had a successful corporate career in telecommunications sales and sales management. At one point, my job was selling exclusively to network marketing companies. Even though I knew many people who had seen great success within the industry, I never considered it to be a good fit for me.

All of that changed with the birth of my daughter and three years later, my son. My priorities shifted and the importance of balance and flexibility in my life became clear to me.

I wanted to experience both personal and professional success without feeling like I had to sacrifice one for the other.

At the time that I was re-introduced to network marketing, I was looking for something but I didn't know what that something was. It was my sponsor's incredible vision that helped me see that this opportunity could be the game-changer for my family and me. She instilled in me the company's professionalism and incredible culture of support. Then she introduced me to the products, and I instantly fell in love!

Today, not only have I replaced my corporate income while working part time from home, but I have fit my business into my life. I get to volunteer for the things that are important to me and I am present in my kids' lives. They see me setting goals and achieving them by helping other people to do the same. They are watching, learning, and already following my lead. Having someone believe in you is the most powerful thing in the world.

Like most people, I started a network marketing business to improve my own situation. But as our business grows, so do we—and something wonderful happens: we become even more successful as we help others succeed, creating an incredible pay-it-forward system and culture of personal growth and development.

The industry shows people how to face their fears, dream

out loud again, and become better versions of themselves.

Suzanne's Words of Wisdom

If you want more out of life, know you can have it. To be successful in this industry simply requires the courage to get started and the discipline to be a good student. The skills will come, as will the belief in yourself. The key is to keep putting one foot in front of the other and not let the temporary setbacks hold you back for life.

Jackie Christiansen, Flip-Flop CEO

Business Owner
Personal Trainer & Sports Nutritionist
Social Media Expert
Network Marketer

Ever hear of an anti-network marketer? That person who always says no to the opportunity, meeting, party, or product...well, that was me. I thought network marketing was one of *those* things and stayed away at all costs. Fast forward a few decades and here I am in the wonderful world of network marketing and at the top of the industry.

What unlocked my thinking and preconceived notions after saying no for so long? Someone asked me for help with a referral for her expanding network marketing business. While helping her, I learned about the stellar nutritional products, and an opportunity that offered unlimited income potential with no geographical boundaries. Because I had previously been in outside sales, I recognized how extraordinary this opportunity was. I already owned a successful business as a personal trainer, but I realized I was trading each hour of the day for money. I knew first hand that *no work* meant *no pay*, so if I got sick, injured, or just wanted to take some time off, the income would stop flowing, and it was taking a toll on my body.

Passive income? Residual income? What was that? I learned quickly that it's a very good thing. The challenge was, I had no experience in network marketing and was unwilling to approach my friends and family. I decided to talk to practically everyone I met while I was out and about. Being the one in our family who ran all the errands helped me to start making money! By consistently building the business in the small increments of time I had each day, I replaced my six-figure income in less than a year. In the second year, I replaced my aerospace engineer husband's income, so he was able to retire at 49.

Does network marketing work? It does if you do! I've built organizations in over twenty countries in the last seven years by meeting incredible people, mostly online. It's not just what you do, but the ability to help others, that makes this business so great. If you love people, enjoy business, and have a passion and drive to achieve greatness, then this is your industry. Do you want to be able to provide for your family, put your kids through college, and donate to the causes and people that touch your heart? This is the arena where it can be done, and on a level playing field, no matter what your background. When your motivation is helping others, there's no stopping you.

Jackie's Words of Wisdom

Make a decision and go for it. Don't stop until you've reached your goals, and then help others reach *their* goals. This is the fastest way to be successful in network marketing because by helping others build their dreams, you'll prosper too. Make personal development a priority and part of your normal routine because as you become better personally, your business will reflect that. Don't *ever* quit. Lastly, but most importantly, thank God daily for the blessings in your life, no matter how big or small they might be—having an attitude of gratitude is a powerful force.

Chris and Amme Weilert, Flip-Flop CEOs

Chris: BBA, Marketing; MBA, Marketing & Finance
Former RV Dealership Owner
Amme: BS, Education
Elementary School Teacher
Network Marketers

Our journey together in network marketing started, when Amme received a call from a childhood friend that included eight magical words, "Do you want to quit your teaching job?" So desperate for a change of career, she jumped in immediately with both feet. Unfortunately, Chris was her biggest skeptic. His exact words were, "That is embarrassing! I own a large company in this town and I don't want my wife being known as the lipstick lady!"

Within six months, Amme replaced her teaching income, and within thirteen months she received her free Mercedes. Twenty-four months after starting, she was at the top level of the company and was earning double the income her husband was making as the owner of his own successful business.

Chris realized several things within that two-year span. He looked at his beautiful wife; she was happy, she loved what she was doing, she was making a high six-figure residual income, and the best part was that she literally worked half the time he did.

At that point, Chris decided he needed to swallow his pride and "get over himself." He'd always thought having multiple degrees and owning a large company was the true path to owning your life, but the truth was—his company owned him—and he was miserable, stressed, and worn out every day. Chris had needed proof. He just couldn't believe that network marketing would really work. But Amme had not only proved him wrong tenfold, but she ultimately had saved him from living a very stressful life.

Chris decided it was time to apologize to Amme. He asked if he could join her "lipstick business" and sold his company.

They have been working as a powerful partnership for almost a decade now. This industry has truly created time and financial freedom for them.

Chris and Amme now have two small children, and this business has allowed them both to be home every day, not missing a single second.

They are growing their empire in other countries with tens of thousands of consultants, and do it from their iPads while watching Mickey Mouse Clubhouse with their boys!

Amme and Chris's Words of Wisdom

Understand this business takes time to build! This is not a get rich quick industry; it's about creating wealth. The only way to fail is to quit, so commit to never quit.

Our industry is so much about timing for people. Life happens to all of us, but it's what you do with life while it's happening to you that will determine your success. Do something for your business EVERY DAY! Whether it is literally five minutes a day, or three-plus hours a day, FIT IT IN!

Action and activity are always better than planning to "make something happen." Daily activity will form a habit of success and take you to the TOP in this business.

Don't wait to GIVE BACK! You don't have to wait until you have achieved ultimate financial and time freedom to make a difference.

Get started now, and find your passion. Passion helps fuel the bigger picture, and will lead you to even bigger dreams. It is about the difference you make philanthropically along your journey that sets you up for bigger things later in life.

Karen Doerflein, Flip-Flop CEO

BA, Business; BSN, Nursing
Small Business Owner
Network Marketer

When I was first introduced to network marketing, I was working eighty hours a week, running three businesses that my husband and I owned. Our three children were five, four, and one year old. While we were financially blessed, we had no quality of life.

The business model of network marketing made complete sense to me, so I signed up the day I was introduced! Once I realized that I did not have to live in the "rat race," constantly working to create the level of income we were used to making, I had no doubts about my decision.

I dove in head first, putting in about six to eight hours a week. With the income I was able to create with network marketing, coupled with the fact that our other companies were being hit so hard by the poor economy, I decided I no longer wanted to be "owned" by a business. I decided to shut down our three high-end cabinet companies. Now I never miss my kids' field trips, my family is able to spend more time together, and my goals and dreams have expanded—all because of network marketing.

The fact that we can impact people's lives while changing our own lives is priceless. Network marketing has made me dream bigger. I want to make an impact by traveling the world, helping build schools and orphanages while showing our children how we can impact others' lives. The freedom network marketing brings is amazing! We are scheduled to move to Bali for a year. It's exciting to know that this business can and will take you around the world if you want it to.

Karen's Words of Wisdom

Don't prejudge anyone and know that we have a gift in our hands to change people's lives. People are praying for an opportunity like this. Give this business at least three years and finish what you set out to do. The world needs more leaders and our children are watching our every move, so make a move worth remembering.

Tina Beer,
Flip-Flop CEO
Flight Attendant
Network Marketer

When I discovered network marketing more than thirteen years ago, I was working full time as a flight attendant, was newly married, and was the primary caregiver for my beloved grandmother, Pearl.

As my grandmother's health declined, there were additional medical expenses that arose each month and we found ourselves getting further and further behind. The smallest unexpected expense like a flat tire or a high electricity bill would devastate our budget for the month. I began praying for something that would give me an opportunity to supplement my income.

Then, one day, while cleaning the seat-back pocket of the aircraft, my prayers were answered when I found a network marketing company's catalog. The catalog had two words on the back that spoke to me: "Income Opportunity." I knew I needed more income and I was open and hungry for an opportunity to change my life.

I didn't fully understand what network marketing was

at the time. And I hadn't ever thought about the concepts of "residual income" and "time leveraging" when I first joined the company. However, the business model itself made complete sense to me and for the very first time in my adult life, I had a deep sense of hope.

I was blessed to have two incredible mentors who shared their wisdom with me and educated me about the value and integrity of this profession. I began my journey fully aware that it would take three to five years of consistent, committed effort to build a solid foundation for my network marketing business, and I embraced it!

I'm truly the perfect example of someone who joined the profession with a need for supplemental income, and by consistently investing my time, I started earning enough to replace my flight attendant income, and eventually created enough to completely change our lifestyle.

This profession has blessed me with so much more than just financial rewards. My husband and I now enjoy living our dreams by design, rather than by default. In my opinion, you cannot put a price tag on having both time and financial freedom. Most people have one or the other. Being able to create a lifestyle that is built around your values and what you hold most important is priceless.

We have evolved in our lives from "we wish we could give" to "we CAN give." And to us, there is nothing more meaningful than being able to bless others through our blessings.

Tina's Words of Wisdom

"Commitment" comes before "results" both in the dictionary and in network marketing. Commit to giving your business the time, space, and grace to grow. Most people overestimate what they can accomplish in one year and hugely underestimate what they can accomplish in five years.

Eileen Williams & Ashley Williams, Flip-Flop CEOs

Eileen: BBA Business USD
Human Resources Mgmt. Consultant
Mom
Ashley: BS, Mass Communication
Network Marketers

Eileen

My parents were incredible examples: they taught me the importance of having a dream, being creative, and working like crazy to achieve it. After college, I worked with my dad at the company he'd created. The experience was more valuable than an MBA. As treasurer, I learned so much about what works and what doesn't in business. Eventually, though, my passion for helping people led me to a career in human resources, and later into consulting for startup technology companies. I really enjoyed the challenge of getting a business off the ground.

My career has always been important to me, and so has being a mom. Once I started having children, they immediately became my greatest treasure, but I didn't want to have to choose between having a happy family and having a successful career. As a working mom, I began to feel more and more frustrated with the demands of the corporate world. I remember crying myself to sleep at night, praying for a way to be there for my kids and yet still have a successful career. I refused to believe that I had to make a choice between the two. I wanted it all!

When my third child was born, I realized that it was time to find a different type of career path. Although I was highly skeptical of the network marketing industry, I was very intrigued by the concept of creating an income stream by leading teams of independent contractors. The flexibility was also very attractive, especially with more and more people looking for a way to have the freedom to be good parents, have a career, and still have a life. So although I didn't quite understand the business, I decided to trust my intuition and joined the network marketing industry. I feel very fortunate that I was introduced to a company with standards that aligned with my own core values.

I am still with the same company today, but my journey was not an easy one. For twelve years I worked my business part time, while continuing to do human resources consulting. I struggled to find success. My children witnessed lots of disappointment and frustration. Thankfully, though, I had made a firm commitment that I would never quit, no matter what.

In 2003 everything changed. My daughter was off to college in Oregon, and I was about to enter a whole new chapter of my life. Our company was about to launch a new technology, and while attending our annual convention I experienced my defining moment. I decided that day to finally be willing to do whatever it took to reach the top.

In the next three years, my business completely exploded and today extends all over the world. The best part is that during all of this growth and personal development, my children were watching me. Today my daughter works with me, and it is so rewarding to know that the dream I had of creating a lifestyle including both a happy family and a fulfilling career is possible! My own experience allows me to help people all over the world create the same thing!

Ashley

My mom started her network marketing business when I was five years old, and did it on a very part time basis until I was seventeen. Our family loved the products and loved the company, but we didn't really understand anything about the business.

When I left for college, I saw my mom transform herself

into an amazing, successful leader. She developed a large network all over the world and completely changed the financial future of our family.

When I was a junior in college studying to be a sports broadcaster, my counselor informed me that to get started I would need to move to a small town. This was not something I wanted to do. I'd always wanted to live in southern California where I grew up. I spent some time journaling about my dreams and what I wanted my life to look like, and what I discovered was that I wanted the exact same thing my mom had created. I wanted to have a family and a career that would provide financial freedom. I wanted to have it all.

That's when I realized that this vehicle called network marketing was the only way to achieve the life I dreamed of. I called my mom and told her I wanted to work with her and be mentored by her after I graduated. It was the most important decision I have ever made. I am so grateful that, on a daily basis, I get to work with my best friend, my hero— my mom. I truly believe that my mom's courage to make her dreams come true created the space for me to believe that my dreams could come true, too. My mom is truly building a legacy as she teaches me how to build a network around the world. We are having so much fun working our businesses together as we mentor others from around the world do the same thing.

Eileen's Words of Wisdom

Trust your inner voice. Walk your path in faith and never give up on your dream. Know that you are here to make a difference—not just exist. The world needs your leadership, and now is the time to be the person you are destined to be.

Ashley's Words of Wisdom

Only listen to people who have the life you want. Don't judge or compare yourself to anyone; we are all on our own journey. Have the courage to go for your dreams and make a difference in the world. Think of the perfect person you want to work with, and become that person. You will attract who you are. You will have good days and bad days, but whatever you do, NEVER QUIT.

kathleen Deggelman, Flip-Flop CEO
BA, Liberal Arts
Real Estate Top Earner
Entrepreneur, Investor, Philanthropist
Network Marketer

After working for other people in Corporate America for more than twenty years, I realized I needed to break free and start my own business. I didn't want a boss or to be on someone else's schedule. I love to travel and I wanted to take lots of vacations! After leaving the corporate world, my first venture was in real estate. Although I achieved success as a top-producing agent, I knew something was missing. I was in my early 40s and didn't want to spend the rest of my life doing what I was doing.

I wanted to become an entrepreneur and began exploring buying a franchise or starting my own business. Along the way, I became passionate about financial literacy and knew I wanted to help others gain control over their finances, too.

In 2006, the real estate market became even scarier, and I knew I needed to quickly find an additional way to make money. I am so grateful that I didn't buy the franchise or start my own business. I found everything I was looking for and more in network marketing. From the beginning, I fell in love with the business model. I said yes right away and I have never looked back. My husband told me recently that I was born to do this. I can't express how wonderful it feels to be doing what you're meant to do.

I immediately recognized that network marketing could give me the kind of financial and personal freedom I wanted, along with the opportunity to make a significant impact in other people's lives. I jumped in and went to work, and have been a top income earner in our profession for the past ten years.

Today, I have a multimillion dollar distributorship consisting of over 70,000 distributors in over 50 countries, and I've helped many others achieve financial freedom—which is one of the things I love most about this business!

On a personal note, I found my husband in this business, too. Everything in my life has changed because I said yes to network marketing. At a company event, I was on stage speaking, and Mark was in the audience. He turned to his sister and said, "I hope I get to tell her someday how much I loved listening to her." We were married a couple of years later. Along with my husband came three great children so I also have the family I've always wanted. We live a wonderful lifestyle free from financial stress, and I've found a way to help people while traveling the world. You couldn't ask for a better profession!

kathleen's words of wisdom

My favorite quote is from Zig Ziglar: "Help enough people get what they want and you will get everything you want." This is why network marketing works! It's all about coming from a place of service and asking, "How can I help you?" When you aren't attached to the outcome and make this about them, you'll be amazed at the results. This business is just like any other; you need to learn the skills and stay consistent. Starting over time and again is the hardest way to build this. Choose well so you can build a career. I wish you great success!

Kanesha Morrison,
Flip-Flop CEO
AA, Early Childhood Education
Professional Job Hopper
Network Marketer

If someone had told me when I was eighteen, that in just a few short years, I would have a testimony to rival that of my idols, I would never have believed you.

Seven years ago, I was pregnant, unemployed, and lost. I didn't know how I was going to care for my baby or what I was going to do with my life. I had no dreams and no goals. Everything I tried always seemed to end in failure.

Then two years later, I was pregnant again. I was still jumping in and out of jobs, trying to find myself and what I wanted to do. My husband was a great support, but I wanted—no, *needed*—to be able to stand on my own two feet.

I felt like I was always stuck between a rock and a hard place. I ended up quitting school with only one year left to get my bachelor's degree. Now 22, I was pregnant with our third child, and had a husband who was tired of wasting money funding my dreams. I was sick of failing, and so frustrated that I had to constantly worry about how I was going to pay the bills. I just wanted freedom and felt like there had to be a way. There was nothing else to do but turn to God. I looked at myself in the mirror and said, "I refuse to let anything stop me. Not even me. I need you, Lord."

I joined *another* network marketing business. But this time my motivation to continue wasn't just about the money; it was about finishing something I had started. I was determined to prove to myself *and* my husband that his money wasn't going to waste. I wanted to show other women that no matter how many mistakes we've made, we can still come out a winner. I didn't care if it was going to take me ten years to do it—I was not going to quit until I achieved success.

Now I barely recognize that eighteen-year-old version of myself. I was so broken and confused, and had no blueprint for how to create the life I so desperately wanted. Today I have four boys and it's *my* income that provides for my family. My success with network marketing has allowed my husband to be at home and pursue his passion. I'm the leader of a team of 26,000 people that is growing daily.

I have made my share of mistakes. I have cried many nights. I have wanted to give up, but, thankfully, I never did.

Kanesha's Words of Wisdom

Once you make up your mind that you'll be successful, nothing can stop you.

**Amanda Schneider,
Flip Flop CEO**
BS, Business Administration
Masters of Arts in Teaching
Network Marketer

"Noooo! It's one of *those* things!" were my exact words as I sat next to my husband googling this great product that had been recommended earlier that day. I had been *so* excited about it until then. I grew up during a time when Ponzi schemes and pyramids were often associated with network marketing. I desperately wanted the product for my family, but the only way to get it was to buy it from this company. Even worse, becoming a representative of this network marketing company was the way to get it at the best price. I wondered if I would be able to overcome the idea of getting involved in "one of *those* things."

I was raised in a home where it was considered noble to pursue a profession helping others for as little money as possible. Much to my father's chagrin, I ended up majoring in business and joined the corporate world. After tiring of corporate politics and working to benefit shareholders, I headed back to school to earn a master's degree in teaching.

I wanted to make a bigger difference in the world. I ended up teaching marketing. I enjoyed helping my students become better educated consumers. The trouble was, I was very biased against MLMs. I believed they were pyramid schemes, with a few people getting rich by recruiting others to do all of the work, while they sat back and did nothing. In spite of the fact that I had absolutely no personal experience or evidence to justify my beliefs, this is what I taught my students. Unfortunately, many people are still doing this. People accept the myths without bothering to do the research. My own ignorance caused me to do a major disservice to my students and to this profession.

Thankfully I believed in the product enough to set aside my pride, and joined the business so that I could purchase the products at a discount. Soon after, I agreed to attend a leadership conference that my sponsor invited me to. That conference changed everything. I still remember the defining moment when I *knew* this was what I was called to do. I'm so thankful I finally decided to look at the business with open eyes. My efforts now benefit those I care most deeply about: My family and my team. I have found a way to make much more of a difference in the world by sharing my passion, and I'm creating a network of people who are doing the same.

There's no limit to my paycheck—it's simply a reflection of the number of people I am impacting. To me, it doesn't get any better than that!

Amanda's Words of Wisdom

Enjoy the journey! This business is about developing you! Attend events and invest in personal development. They keep you connected to your tribe and build belief in your products, company, network marketing, and yourself. And learn to dream again. You *can* make them come true with network marketing!

Hope Baker, Flip-Flop CEO

BA, Journalism, University of Wisconsin
Flight Attendant
Realtor
Personal Trainer
Network Marketer

I was introduced to my company and network marketing in 2005 because, thankfully, I was in the right place at the right time! When I found this business, I was at a turning point in my life. I was a "forty-something" single mom who wanted to create the best life I could for myself and my son. I just couldn't figure out exactly how to do that.

I had several fulfilling careers in my life. After college, I was a flight attendant for many years; I sold real estate and became a personal trainer. Although I enjoyed all of those vocations, my circumstances had changed and those careers didn't fit where I was in my life. I was committed to being the best mom I could be, but also needed to find a career I could be passionate about that would pay me a substantial income to support my family.

I had always felt that there was something more out there—something I hadn't found yet. It was time to stop looking backwards and start looking forward.

I was drawn to this business model for so many reasons. I loved that I could represent products I believed in, I loved that this business model provides a win-win for everyone involved, and I loved the opportunity it offered, both personally and financially.

After doing my due diligence, I discovered that network marketing is nothing short of brilliant. I realized that, through word of mouth advertising, I could share something I believed in, help change people's lives, and get paid to do something that didn't feel like "work"!

I recognized that network marketing would allow me to live my life by design. I saw that my company and the industry could give me freedom and choices in my life that nothing else could. I saw that it would allow me to make a difference, not only to myself and my family, but to others as well!

Today, I have a multi-million dollar business that I run from my kitchen table. I am paid an income that allows my son and me to live our dreams. But this business means so much more than that. Because I found this industry, I get to live my life first, and build my career around my life! I have been the hands-on mother that I so wanted to be, attending not just my son's school functions and games, but traveling the world with him and giving him opportunities that I could have only dreamed of.

I have a passion and a purpose and love Mondays as much as the weekends. While other people my age are starting to worry about retiring, I have peace of mind and nothing but hope for the future. Maybe best of all, because I found this business, my sixteen-year-old son sees no limits in his future and knows that absolutely anything is possible. That is one of the many gifts that network marketing has given to my family.

Hope's Words of Wisdom

Network marketing means different things to different people, but I truly believe—now more than ever—that it is the perfect vehicle to make our dreams a reality.

Sue Cassidy, Flip-Flop CEO
College Dropout
Model, Songwriter
Network Marketer

Before I began my network marketing business, I was a college dropout. On a whim, I moved to England where I became a professional model and self-taught songwriter.

Over the years, I wrote songs for artists including Smokey Robinson, Meatloaf, Cher, and Michael Jackson and earned a Grammy nomination for my contribution to Tina Turner's *Private Dancer* album,

I lived a life most people would consider to be a "dream" life. After moving back to the States, I married a high-profile person in the entertainment industry and we had a beautiful son. I was an instrument-rated pilot, an author, and the founder of a worldwide children's charity. So why would I want to be a professional network marketer? Because, I was preparing for impact.

After seventeen years of being a stay-at-home mom, my son was heading off to college. I was a dinosaur in the music business and I was at an age when most people start to retire. I was scared that the best part of my life was behind me.

So when I was introduced to my company, I dragged

myself, kicking and screaming, out of my comfort zone and reinvented myself. It wasn't easy. People thought I was crazy, but I refused to give them a crystal ball for my life just because they didn't have one!

Once I realized that the people who said "no" to me weren't going to pay my bills, I took a leap of faith and landed in the top level of my company within ten months of starting my business.

Owning a network marketing business is the best decision I ever made. I only wish I had been smart enough to understand the industry when I was much younger. The new relationships and lessons I have learned are priceless. Amazingly, many of my former colleagues in the music industry have now joined me in the business as well. We are having fun together dancing to the beat of our own drums and experiencing success all over again in a whole new way.

I was afraid of the future before I began my networking marketing business. Now I have discovered that the best is yet to come! I am living proof that if you make your goals greater than your fears, you can live your dreams.

Sue's Words of Wisdom

Owning a network marketing business is like having

an insurance policy that pays out while you and your loved ones are still alive to enjoy it. Only no one has to get sick or die! You are building an asset that grows over time—that can create wealth beyond your wildest dreams.

Brenda and Scott Schuler, Flip-Flop CEOs

Brenda: BA, Exercise Physiology
Exercise Physiologist
Scott: Doctor of Chiropractic and F.A.S.A
Chiropractor
Network Marketers

I would never have guessed that someone sharing one product with me would eventually change the trajectory of my family's life. In 1999, a coworker shared a product to help me with some digestive issues.

I was afraid to share it with my husband, Scott, because it was from a network marketing company. I had dabbled in network marketing before with no success, so when I told Scott, he thought I had been sucked into another "scam."

We agreed that I would use the product but I wouldn't share it with family or friends (we didn't want to join the "NFL," no friends left).

As time went on, not being able to talk about my success with the products became increasingly difficult because I knew I had discovered something that could change lives.

I started out by giving the products away. Then people started begging me to help them get their own accounts.

The more I learned about the products, the more passionate I became about educating the world about health and alternative medicine.

Our first child was born with significant and very expensive health issues. That situation, coupled with the addition of our second and third children, caused us to find ourselves $100,000 in credit card debt, sitting in an attorney's office ready to file bankruptcy.

Scott and I just couldn't do it. We agreed that after work he would stay at home with the kids, and I would spend five or six nights a week building this business. Eleven months later, we paid off our $100,000 debt. A year after that, Scott retired from his chiropractic practice, and we became partners in the business.

Although our personalities are very different, we've found that our styles complement each other, which has propelled our business forward to new heights and allowed us to both be at home with our kids.

I don't know of any other opportunity that could have changed our lives so dramatically.

I am forever grateful for this incredible business model. It's not only given our family financial freedom, but because we are able to plan our work around our life, we have time freedom, as well. We are living a lifestyle that most only dream about.

Brenda and Scott's Words of Wisdom

None of us are as smart as all of us. Teamwork really does make the dream work! If you are going to embark on this wonderful journey, find a few people you love and adore, and take them with you. As with anything new, realize that when you first start something, you're not going to be that good at it. Just remember that leaders are readers and learners are earners, so invest in yourself and your team and watch the magic happen.

Whitney Husband, Flip Flop CEO

BA, Business Administration
Bank Teller
Network Marketer

I began my career in network marketing at twenty-four years old. After I graduated from college, I started working as a bank teller making $10 an hour. At the time, I was pregnant with my son and began to experience complications with the pregnancy. At 35-weeks pregnant, I was forced to leave my job to take care of my health. After Ayden was born, it was impossible to find a job that would pay me enough money to cover food, daycare, and all of our bills. The best decision at the time was for my family to go on government assistance so I could at least be at home with my baby. We struggled to make ends meet this way for almost two years.

I had dreams but no plan. I went to college because I truly desired to be successful and provide for my family. The moment I became a mom, my drive for success and my need to be home to care for my son quickly caused an internal conflict. If I stayed at home, I felt I should be at a job. If I went to a job, I felt that I should be at home. I never felt I was in the right place. I was lost, depressed, and extremely stressed. I found myself crying all of the time and feeling completely miserable.

Wanting to be home with my son through his first five years was the most important thing to me. This is what made me search for a job I could do from home. I tried lots of different things: Online surveys, referral programs, and I even dipped my toes into network marketing once before, but none of these things gave me any real source of income, or the sense of accomplishment I wanted. It wasn't until I found the right network marketing company for me that I was able to fulfill my drive for success and see the financial rewards I was looking for. I learned very quickly that the key to success in this business is about building others up, and I love that aspect of it the most. I have built a team of people whom I love and respect. I consider them my friends, and they're all experiencing their own successes. Their lives are changing just as mine had, and it fills my heart with joy to be able to witness this every day. This has become a sisterhood of successful, likeminded women. We operate as a team, pushing each other to achieve our dreams.

I have seen firsthand how network marketing can turn dreams of earning a little extra income into a life-changing opportunity. I want to help more moms stay home with their kids.

whitney's words of wisdom

Find your strength through your struggles, and when you do that, you can change your future.

Natalie-Jade Penney, Flip Flop CEO

High School Graduate
Dance Teacher
Accountant
Network Marketer

At 25 years old, I've been a dance teacher, a singer, an actress, and an accountant. Growing up, my dream was to dance professionally as a Disney Princess. It seemed silly to some, but I thought about it constantly. When I was young, I believed I could have anything I set my mind to. Then, one day, I had the opportunity to audition for my dream job. I thought it was *finally* my chance to shine. But instead of shining, fear took over, and instantly my hopes and dreams vanished. Everything I'd ever wanted was suddenly taken away.

I was without a job, my family…and the hope of a better future. I'd somehow lost the focus and control over my life that I'd once had. I felt like I'd never accomplish anything I could be proud of.

As my dreams faded away, my weight spiraled out of control and I lost all self-confidence. As hard as I tried, I couldn't seem to feel positive about anything. Then I saw a

Facebook post and felt as if fate were pulling me towards it. I couldn't stop thinking about it. I grabbed the opportunity with both hands! Now, three years later, I can't imagine being any happier.

I'd heard of work-from-home opportunities but never really believed they could be as good as they sounded. But, after only six months, I was able to walk away from my career, and no longer had to deal with rejected holiday requests, or worrying if I needed to take time off for an emergency.

This opportunity has given me the gift of time and financial freedom. I'm able to build my business around my life, using my mobile phone and social media while getting my hair done, shopping, or spending time with loved ones.

I'm in the best health I've ever been in, and I've even met my real life Prince Charming in our company. This Christmas I'll get to experience my dream of being a real princess for the day. The moral of the story is to never give up on your dreams, even if you have to take a different path to get to your "happily ever after."

Natalie-Sade's Words of Wisdom

It's OK to be skeptical, but ask yourself: "Can I afford to miss an opportunity of a lifetime?" Everyone has an opinion—both negative and positive people. We also all have a belly button. They're in no way related to one another. The next time a negative person has anything to say about your life choices simply think: "Belly button." I do this, on average, three times a day, and laugh each time. The people with a closed mindset will never be where I am, so why would I ever listen to them?

Be sure to have fun. If you aren't having fun, you aren't doing it right.

Afterword

This book isn't about our stories. It's really about your story, including the parts you've yet to write. But we decided to include a few more details about our individual journeys in this Afterword, so that you get a better idea of where our passion comes from, in case you catch a glimpse of yourself.

Lory (Daughter), Flip-Flop CEO

BA, Interdisciplinary Studies: Marketing
Communications and Spanish
Network Marketer

When I first found out about network marketing, I was shocked. I had no idea that anything like this existed. I was searching for freedom from what everyone else considered to be "the real world." Although I was successful in it, I had zero passion for corporate America. Work was time-consuming and I was miserable. Being fresh out of college and young, I missed my spring breaks, my flip-flops, and waking up without an alarm clock. My dream life was quickly becoming my biggest nightmare. I wanted out.

I began to search for something better. I kept my eyes wide open for other possibilities. I was not opposed to trying something new or different or "outside" the box. In fact, I welcomed it. As long as it took me far away from this lifestyle that I was beginning to resent. Being naive was such a blessing because, looking back, I didn't have any preconceived ideas about this profession. I thought it was brilliant, so I jumped in with both feet.

I quickly discovered the stigma that surrounded network marketing, beginning at home. The one person I wanted to pursue this with was my mom, but she wanted *nothing* to do with it. I couldn't understand how her aversion for a profession could be so strong, when it made so much sense to me. As it turned out, a lot of my friends felt the same way she did. They thought I was crazy. But I thought *they* were crazy. We were gridlocked. And for a while, nothing changed. It was a trying time.

Then, after a year of not seeing any results, my determination to keep going finally paid off. Thank goodness quitting was never an option. When my mom and I finally joined forces, we were unstoppable. We didn't let other people determine our future. We knew what was possible in this business and in life, and we were confident that we could create that for ourselves. Together we were better. Her strengths were my weaknesses, her weaknesses were my strengths. As a team, we were able to reach the top of the company within a year.

No one can tell us that network marketing doesn't work, when we are living proof that it does. I believe this is possible for anyone who wants it. I realize that not everyone wants it. But anyone who does want more choices in their life can have them. They just have to be willing to *go for it*.

I don't believe there is a right or wrong way to live, but I definitely believe it's a choice. We all have choices. Network marketing is not an "either/or"; it's choosing both—time and money, making a difference and making a living, being a mom and a provider.

I love that when I wake up every day, I get to choose how to spend it. How I spend my days is how I spend my life, so having the freedom to live my life on my terms means raising my kids while raising the abundance in this world.

Lory's Words of Wisdom

If you love what you do, keep doing it!! This isn't about quitting your job in order to "do" network marketing. This is about incorporating it into your life and having more choices. Then you can decide what you want to do. Listen to your heart above all other voices, and never ever give up!

Janine (Mother), Flip-Flop CEO
Associate of Arts Degree
Network Marketer

When Lory told me how excited she was about this "new" career that she'd discovered, I thought she was crazy. She had no idea what she was getting herself into. As someone who'd been approached years before in a very secretive and misleading way, I wanted Lory to understand what she was getting into. I believed that the business had *nothing* to do with marketing and *everything* to do with using your relationships with family and friends for personal gain. I wanted no part of it, and I could not see myself, or my daughter, as "one of those people!"

After a year of us battling over our respective truths, I decided to look for a way to show her just how naive she was being, and how absurd it would be to give up the amazing career she'd worked so hard to have. So I began to do my own due diligence. As I did, the opposite outcome occurred. I found out just how much things had transformed over the prior thirty years—changes that took this profession from being an embarrassment to being one of the best opportunities around. I finally "got" it, and realized how bigoted I had been. It was as if my life had suddenly flipped right-side-up, for the very first time.

As they say, what goes around, comes around. So the second I shifted my paradigm, I was faced with skepticism and hurtful judgments by the people in *my* life. It was a challenging time for me. Some days it still is. But I know that I could never go back to working for someone else's dream again. All those years that I struggled as a single mom and couldn't be there for my girls because I was working, I get to do differently today with my grandchildren. Now that I've discovered a business that I can work around my priorities, I never feel like I'm *working*.

As a stay-at-home grandma, I get to be at every "mom's group" activity, enjoy long lunches with my girlfriends, and take trips with my daughters whenever we want to. I never have to choose between being there for my family and having a thriving career. It's a freedom and lifestyle that I cannot help but want to share with others.

Network marketing is a way to not only make a great income, but to make a difference as well.

Our business gives us the opportunity to work on ourselves, to become the best people that we can be, and to help others do the same. It's a business founded on empowering others to attain their dreams, with a financial structure attached that rewards you in direct proportion to your accomplishments.

Never has there been a more crucial time to bring clarity and understanding to a model whose time has come.

This business is the *best kept secret* around and now that I've seen the light at the end of the tunnel, I want to be that light for others. We believe it's time to provide some updated information about this profession! We hope our book can provide that.

Janine's Words of Wisdom

If you're not a dreamer naturally, learn to be one. The most valuable thing I've learned these past ten years is the importance of knowing what you want. You don't have to know *how* you'll get there, but you get exactly what you think about. So think about what you want—instead of what you don't want! When your *why* is big enough and clear enough, the *how* will take care of itself!

Whitney (Writer), Flip-Flop CEO

BA, Political Science and Sociology
Juris Doctor
Network Marketer

When I met Lory and Janine, I was a recovering attorney, semi-retired entrepreneur, and freelance writer, taking the occasional gig to bankroll my lazy life at the beach.

I thought I'd done it all. I'd rejected corporate America when I left the practice of law at age twenty-seven; I'd followed my dreams of self-employment when I started a business that ultimately led to greater freedom; and I'd created passive income by self-publishing a textbook that had unexpected success. In my mind, I was everything but a network marketer.

On top of that, I tried to avoid them at all costs. As a business owner, I'd been a member of many different networking organizations and was exhausted from colliding with pushy people who swore that I would get rich quick if I'd just give them five minutes of my time. I never met one person who was rich, let alone quick, and I found the whole thing to be ridiculous.

So when a friend asked me to consider writing a book with Lory and Janine about network marketing, I figured she'd lost her mind. I was *obviously* the wrong person for the job. I mean, it's one thing to hire someone full of sass; it's another to hire someone full of disdain. Besides, I was sure they couldn't afford my fee (I know, so rude).

Nonetheless, I agreed to the meeting because they seemed nice and sincere in their mission to shed light on this profession. Plus, I got the part about the money wrong.

The rest, as they say, is history. After diving into the research on network marketing, my mind wasn't just opened, it was *changed*. I finally "got" the professional side of network marketing, which was so different from the style I'd been exposed to before. On top of that, I couldn't believe how many savvy, sophisticated, and fun people were already doing it with astounding success. Here I was, running to the ends of the Earth looking for financial freedom, and the best option was staring me in the face. Talk about being wrong.

So, without any encouragement from Lory and Janine, I jumped into network marketing while working on the book. When they saw that my belief in the profession had grown as strong as theirs, they invited me to put my name on it, too.

Eight months later, I'm already turning a sizable profit in my network marketing business.

It hasn't always been a breeze, but it's a heck of a lot easier than all the other things I've done.

Like a lot of entrepreneurs, I want a big fat life. I want adventure; I want fun. I want to sample every delicious opportunity that comes my way. Network marketing is the vehicle that makes all of that possible now. I can't believe I almost missed it (ten times).

Today, I no longer think about what I want to do for a living. I think about what I want to do with my life.

Whitney's Words of Wisdom

You're only in this game once. Don't settle for being a spectator.

Get the Facts

- The Direct Selling Association, which also represents network marketing companies, recently celebrated its 100th anniversary. [i]

- As of 2012, 15.9 million people are registered network marketers in the United States. [ii]

- As of 2012, 90 million people are registered network marketers worldwide. [iii]

- United States online retail sales, will grow from $225.5 billion in 2012 to $434.2 billion in 2017. Online retail sales will grow at a compound annual rate of 10% from 2012-2017. [iv]

- In 2012, between "Black Friday" and "Cyber Monday" (the Friday, Saturday and Sunday after Thanksgiving), online sales grew 30.3% from the prior year. 18% of those purchases were made on mobile devices. [v]

Resources

These are some of the books, CDs, websites and people that we love (we think you'll love them too). Additional resources can be found on our website at TheFlipFlopCEO.com.

Dare to Dream, Work to Win, Understanding the Dollars and Sense of Success in Network Marketing, Dr. Tom Barrett

The New Professionals, The Rise of Network Marketing as the Next Major Profession, James A. Robinson and Charles W. King

Think and Grow Rich for Women, Sharon Lechter, 2014

The Business School for People Who Like Helping People, Robert T. Kiyosaki and Sharon L. Lechter, 2005

Brilliant Compensation Audio CD, Tim Sales

The 45-Second Business Presentation that Will Change Your Life, Don Failla, FaillaPublications.com

The Slight Edge, Secret to a Successful Life, Jeff Olson

The Seven Habits of Highly Successful Network Marketing Professionals, Audio CD, Stephen R. Covey

Think and Grow Rich, Napoleon Hill

The Master Key to Riches, Napoleon Hill

The Success Formula, Bob Burg

Networking Times, NetworkingTimes.com

Dave Ramsey, DaveRamsey.com

Endnotes

i   Direct Selling Association, http://www.dsa.org

ii   Direct Selling Association, http://www.dsa.org/research/industry-statistics

iii   World Federation of Direct Selling Associations, http://www.wfdsa.org/press/index.cfm?fa=show_release&Document_id=836

iv   http://www.internetretailer.com/trends/sales

v   http://www.cnbc.com/2015/12/01/cyber-monday-sales-top-3-billion-beat-forecast.html

vi   http://www.esquire.com/news-politics/news/a41147/half-of-americans-less-than-1000/

vii   http://www.marketwatch.com/story/most-americans-are-one-paycheck-away-from-the-street-2016-01-06

viii http://www.uscourts.gov/news/2015/04/27/march-2015-bankruptcy-filings-down-12-percent

ix   The Hackett Group, "Acceleration of Offshoring Trend Driving Loss of Millions of Finance and IT Jobs in U.S. and

Europe," http://www.thehackettgroup.com/about/alerts/
alerts_2010/alert_12022010.jsp, *accessed March 5, 2011*

[x]   http://www.tradingeconomics.com/united-states/
unemployment-rate

[xi]   http://www.valuepenguin.com/average-credit-card-debt

[xii]   https://www.shrm.org/research/surveyfindings/articles/
pages/job-satisfaction-and-engagement-report-revitalizing-
changing-workforce.aspx

[xiii]   *The New York Times*, "Job Losses in City Reach Up Ladder,"
http://www.nytimes.com/2008/12/12/nyregion/12jobs.html,
accessed March 5, 2011

[xi]   http://www.forbes.com/sites/susanadams/2012/05/18/new-
survey-majority-of-employees-dissatisfied

[xiv]   https://studentloanhero.com/student-loan-debt-
statistics-2016/

[xv]   http://www.bloomberg.com/news/articles/2016-03-10/why-
you-shouldn-t-worry-about-rising-auto-loan-debt

[xvi]   http://www.valuepenguin.com/average-credit-card-debt

xvii   https://studentloanhero.com/student-loan-debt-
statistics-2016/

xviii http://www.forbes.com/sites/moneybuilder/2013/02/01/
alarming-numberof-student-loans-are-delinquent

xix   Michael Gerber, *The E-Myth Revisited*, 2

xx   http://nvca.org/pressreleases/58-8-billion-in-venture-
capital-invested-across-u-s-in-2015-according-to-the-
moneytree-report-2/

xxi   *Bloomberg BusinessWeek*, "Social Security Is Solid: Despite
talk of a need for privatization, the U.S. government
program still does the job and requires only modest tweaks:
Pro or Con?" http://www.businessweek.com/debateroom/
archives/2007/12/social_security_is_solid.html, *accessed
March 5, 2011*

xxii Maddy Dychtwald, Influence, 150-151

xxiii *TheWashington Times*, "Both parties mull raising the
retirement age," http://www.washingtontimes.com/
news/2010/jul/13/both-parties-mull-raisingretirement-age,
accessed March 5, 2011

xxiv http://www.marketplace.org/2015/08/03/economy/many-boomers-cant-afford-retire

xxv http://www.bls.gov/news.release/volun.nr0.htm

xxvi http://www.pay-equity.org/

xxvii http://kff.org/other/state-indicator/life-expectancy-by-gender/

xxiii http://www.drweil.com/drw/u/QAA401207/Why-Do-Women-Live-Longer-than-Men.html

xxix http://www.businessweek.com/news/2012-07-25/women-seen-livingretirement-in-poverty-at-higher-rates-than-men

xxx http://www.singleparentcenter.net/single-parent-statistics.html

xxxi https://singlemotherguide.com/single-mother-statistics/

xxxii Maddy Dychtwald, Influence, 147, as referenced in *The New York Times*, "Mothers Bearing a Second Burden," May 14, 1989

All truth passes through three stages.
First, it is ridiculed.
Second, it is violently opposed.
Third, it is accepted as being self-evident.

Arthur Schopenhauer

Share the Flip-Flop Lifestyle!

Share the flip-flop lifestyle with family, friends, teammates, and everyone you know who is so *over* alarm clocks, bosses, and cubicles! Make a list of people who need to learn about network marketing and then circulate this book when you're done with it.

_____

_____

_____

_____

_____

_____

_____

_____

_____

_____

_____

_____

_____

Join the Movement!

Please join our *movement*, visit our Facebook page, and help spread the word that it IS possible to live your life by design!

To help you share this book with others, bulk discounts are available on our website at **TheFlipFlopCEO.com**

PS. We love feedback. Please feel free to write a review on Amazon.com.